Netherlands Antilles

The People, History and Cultural differences, Tourism

Author
Stephen Dean

Copyright Notice

Copyright © 2017 Global Print Digital
All Rights Reserved

Digital Management Copyright Notice. This Title is not in public domain, it is copyrighted to the original author, and being published by **Global Print Digital**. No other means of reproducing this title is accepted, and none of its content is editable, neither right to commercialize it is accepted, except with the consent of the author or authorized distributor. You must purchase this Title from a vendor who's right is given to sell it, other sources of purchase are not accepted, and accountable for an action against. We are happy that you understood, and being guided by these terms as you proceed. Thank you

First Printing: 2017.

ISBN: 978-1-912483-10-5

Publisher: Global Print Digital.
Arlington Row, Bibury, Cirencester GL7 5ND
Gloucester
United Kingdom.
Website: www.homeworkoffer.com

Table of Content

Introduction 1
    Land 3
    Drainage and soils 4
    Climate 5
    Plant and animal life 5

People and Culture 7
    Social Stratification 9
    Gender Roles and Statuses 9
    Marriage, Family, and Kinship 10
    Socialization 11
    Etiquette 12
    Religion 12
    Medicine and Health Care 13
    Secular Celebrations 14
    The Arts and Humanities 14
    National cuisine of Netherlands Antilles 16
    Cultural Life 18

Food and Economy 22

History 26
    Colonial rule 26
    Political developments since World War II 29
    Government and Society 32

Territories 33
    Bonaire 33
        Bonaire's history 33
        Bonaire Government & Economy 37
        Bonaire's Culture 39
        Tourism 40
            Travel Guide 40
            Things to Do 41
            Attractions 44
            Shopping and Leisure 47
            Transportation 49
            Airports 50
            Travel Tips 52
            Visas and Vaccinations 54
            Festivals and Events 55
            Restaurants 58

- Travel Tips ... 60
- Entry Requirements ... 66
- Accommodation ... 71
  - Hotels ... 71
  - Hotels and Resorts ... 71
  - Bonaire Intimate Hotels and Resorts (Guesthouses, B&B) ... 75
- Weather ... 76

Curacao ... 79
- History of Curaçao ... 79
- Economy & Government ... 83
  - Government ... 83
  - Economy ... 84
- Travel and Tourism ... 85
  - Travel Guide ... 85
  - Things to Do ... 87
  - Attractions ... 90
  - Food and Restaurants ... 94
  - Shopping and Leisure ... 96
  - Culture: sights to visit ... 98
  - Traditions & lifestyle ... 100
  - Nightlife ... 102
  - Transportation ... 103
  - Airports ... 105
  - Visas and Vaccinations ... 107
  - Weather ... 108
  - Holidays and Festivals ... 110

Saba ... 114
- History & Culture ... 114
- Travel and Tourism ... 118
  - Travel Guide ... 118
  - Things to Do ... 121
  - Attractions ... 123
  - Food and Restaurants ... 127
  - Shopping and Leisure ... 129
  - Transportation ... 131
  - Airports ... 132
  - Travel Tips ... 133
  - Visas and Vaccinations ... 135
  - Weather ... 136
  - Holidays and Festivals ... 138
  - Travel information ... 140

    Saba Road 145
    Saba Port 148
St. Eustatius 151
  St. Eustatius History 151
  Tourism 154
    Travel Guide 154
    Things to Do 156
    Attractions 158
    Food and Restaurants 161
    Shopping and Leisure 164
    Transportation 166
    Airports 167
    Travel Tips 168
    Visas and Vaccinations 170
    Weather 172
    Holidays and Festivals 174
Sint Maarten 176
  History and Culture 177
  History 177
    Culture 179
  Travel and Tourism 180
    Travel Guide 180
    Things to Do 182
    Attractions 184
    Holidays and Festivals 187
    Food and Restaurants 189
    Shopping and Leisure 191
    Transportation 193
    Airports 195
    Travel Tips 196
    Visas and Vaccinations 198
    Weather 200

Introduction

Netherlands Antilles, or Dutch Nederlandse Antillen, Papiamentu Antianan Hulandes, are group of five islands in the Caribbean Sea that formerly constituted an autonomous part of the Kingdom of the Netherlands. The group is composed of two widely separated subgroups approximately 500 miles (800 km) apart. The southern group comprises Curaçao and Bonaire, which lie less than 50 miles (80 km) off the Venezuelan coast. The northern group is made up of Sint Eustatius, Saba, and Sint Maarten (the southern part of the island of Saint Martin; the northern part, Saint-Martin, is an overseas collectivity of France). Although the northern islands are locally referred to as "Windward," they lie within the Leeward Islands group of the Lesser Antilles chain. The capital and largest city was Willemstad, on Curaçao.

After 1954 the Netherlands Antilles were an integral part of the Netherlands, with full autonomy in internal affairs. The island of

Aruba, which lies to the west of Curaçao and Bonaire, had initially been part of the Netherlands Antilles, but in 1986 it seceded from the federation to become a separate Dutch territory. In 2006 the Dutch government and the remaining five islands agreed to dissolve the Netherlands Antilles within the following several years. The event took place on October 10, 2010. None of the islands chose full independence. Curaçao and Sint Maarten became autonomous countries within the kingdom, a status similar to that of Aruba. Bonaire, Saba, and Sint Eustatius became special municipalities with closer relations to the central government, similar to those of the municipalities in the Netherlands proper. This article discusses the Netherlands Antilles as a historical entity as it existed at the time of its dissolution.

Demography. Curaçao, the largest and most populated of the islands, had a population of 153,664 in 1997. Bonaire had 14,539 inhabitants. For Sint Maarten, Sint Eustatius, and Saba the population figures were 38,876, 2,237, and 1,531 respectively. As a result of industrialization, tourism, and migration, Curaçao, Bonaire, and Sint Maarten are multicultural societies. On Sint Maarten, migrants outnumber the indigenous island population. Economic recession has caused a growing migration to the Netherlands; the number of Antilleans living there is close to 100,000.

Linguistic Affiliation. Papiamentu is the local language of Curaçao and Bonaire. Caribbean English is the language of the SSS islands. The official language is Dutch, which is spoken little in daily life.

The origins of Papiamentu are much debated, with two views prevalent. According to the monogenetic theory, Papiamentu, like other Caribbean Creole languages, originated from a single Afro-Portuguese proto-creole, that developed as a lingua franca in western Africa in the days of the slave trade. The polygenetic theory maintains that Papiamentu developed in Curaçao on a Spanish base.

Symbolism. On 15 December 1954, the islands obtained autonomy within the Dutch kingdom, and this is the day the Antilles commemorates the unity of the Dutch Kingdom. The Dutch royal family was an important point of reference to the Antillean nation before and directly after World War II.

The Antillean flag and anthem express the unity of the island group; the islands have their own flags, anthems, and coats of arms. Insular festive days are more popular than national festivities.

Land

Relief

The southern islands are generally low in elevation, though hills rise to 787 feet (240 metres) at Brandaris on Bonaire and 1,230 feet (375 metres) at Mount Saint Christoffel on Curaçao. The islands consist mainly of igneous rocks and are fringed with coral reefs. The northern islands consist of volcanic rocks rising to 1,119 feet (341 metres) at Sentry Hill in the Dutch part of Saint Martin, 1,198 feet (365 metres) at The Quill, an extinct volcano on Sint Eustatius, with a large forested crater, and 2,910 feet (887 metres) at Mount Scenery, an extinct volcano on Saba that is the islands' highest point.

Curaçao, the largest island of the Netherlands Antilles, covers 171 square miles (444 square km). It is indented in the south by deep bays, the largest of which, Schottegat, provides a magnificent harbour for Willemstad. Bonaire, with an area of 111 square miles (288 square km), lies about 20 miles (32 km) east of Curaçao. Sint Eustatius covers 8 square miles (21 square km) and Saba 5 square miles (13 square km); the two form the northwestern terminus of the inner volcanic arc of the Lesser Antilles. Saba is dominated by Mount Scenery and is surrounded by sea cliffs. The villages of The Bottom and Windward Side, occupying an old crater, are approached by a steep road from a rocky landing place on the southern coast.

Drainage and soils

For the most part, the islands have barren soil and little or no fresh water. On Curaçao and Bonaire there is much bare, eroded soil, the result of centuries of overgrazing. Drinking water on these islands is obtained mainly by distilling seawater.

Climate

Temperatures in the southern islands vary little from an annual average in the low 80s F (about 27 °C), and the heat is tempered by the easterly trade winds. The islands lie west of the usual tropical cyclone (hurricane) zone. Precipitation in the south is low and variable, often less than 22 inches (550 mm) per year. The climate is similar in the northern islands, but there is more precipitation, and hurricanes are more common. The annual precipitation is greatest on Sint Eustatius and Saba, which receive averages of about 42 inches (1,000 mm) and 47 inches (1,200 mm), respectively, mainly between May and November.

Plant and animal life

The vegetation of the southern islands has been much overgrazed by livestock. Cacti and other drought-resistant plants abound. The island of Bonaire is known for its flamingos. Curaçao has many reptiles, including geckos, lizards, and sea turtles. In the northern group, Saba is noted particularly for its pristine beauty and tropical rainforest; orchids, tree ferns, and wildflowers are abundant, and the island's sea life includes barracudas, sharks, sea turtles, and coral gardens.

People and Culture

The islands' populations are mainly composed of "blacks" (people of African heritage) and mulattos (mixed African and European heritage) except for Saba's, which is about evenly divided between people of African and of European ("white") descent. Most of the islands have small white minorities. Migration to Curaçao from other Caribbean islands, Venezuela, and Europe increased after the opening of its oil refinery in 1918.

The official languages are English, Dutch, and Papiamentu, a local Spanish-based creole that includes Portuguese, Dutch, and some African words. Papiamentu is widely used in the southern islands and is taught in elementary schools. English is the principal language of the northern islands and is widely spoken in Curaçao as well; Spanish is also spoken in the south. Nearly three-fourths of the people adhere to Roman Catholicism; about one-sixth are Protestant; and there are small minorities of Spiritists, Buddhists, and Jews. Curaçao has a

Sephardic Jewish community that dates from the 1650s; Willemstad has the oldest synagogue in continuous use in the Western Hemisphere.

The birth and death rates are relatively low, and the rate of natural increase is lower than on most other islands of the Caribbean. Migration to the Netherlands has tended to increase during economic downturns in the islands, such as during the late 1990s and the early 21st century. Life expectancy is in the mid-70s for males and the late 70s for females.

About four-fifths of the population is urban. The rural population of the islands is generally dispersed, and villages are scarce except on Saba. Nearly three-fourths of the inhabitants of the islands reside on Curaçao; the next two most-populous are Sint Maarten and Bonaire. Sint Eustatius and Saba account for a statistically tiny portion of the population. However, they are more densely settled than Bonaire. Sint Maarten has the highest population density.

Characteristic of Curaçao are its landhuizen, large 18th- and 19th-century rural mansions located on hills. Willemstad has some splendid sections of Dutch-style colonial architecture with tropical adaptations, painted in white and pastel colours.

Social Stratification

Classes and Castes. In all the islands, racial, ethnic, and economic stratification are intertwined. On Saba, the relationship between black and white inhabitants is comfortable. On Curaçao, racial and economic stratification are more obvious. Unemployment is high among the Afro-Curaçaoan population. Trade minorities of Jewish, Arabian, and Indian descent and foreign investors have their own positions in the socioeconomic structure. Curaçao, Sint Maarten, and Bonaire have many immigrants from Latin America and the Caribbean, who hold the lowest positions in the tourism and construction sectors.

Symbols of Social Stratification. Luxury goods such as cars and houses express social status. In traditional celebrations of important life events such as birthdays and First Communion, conspicuous consumption takes place. The middle classes aspire to upper-class consumption patterns, which often puts pressure on a family's budget.

Gender Roles and Statuses

Division of Labor by Gender. Women's participation in the labor market has increased since the 1950s, but men still hold the most important positions throughout the economy. Women work mostly in sales and as nurses, teachers, and civil servants. Unemployment is higher for women than for men. Since the 1980s, the Antilles has had two female prime ministers and several female ministers. Women from the Caribbean and Latin America work in the tourism sector and as live-in maids.

The Relative Status of Women and Men. Until the 1920s, the upper strata of society, especially on Curaçao, had a highly patriarchal family system in which men had social and sexual freedom and women were subordinate to their spouses and fathers. In the Afro-Antillean population sexual relations between men and women were not enduring and marriage was the exception. Many households had a female head, who often was the chief provider for herself and her children. Men, as fathers, husbands, sons, brothers, and lovers, often made material contributions to more than one household.

Mothers and grandmothers enjoy high prestige. The central role of the mother is keeping the family together, and the strong bond between mother and child is expressed in songs, proverbs, sayings, and expression.

Marriage, Family, and Kinship

Marriage. Couples often marry at an older age because of the matrifocal family type, and the number of illegitimate children is high.

Visiting relationships and extramarital relationships are prevalent, and the number of divorces is growing.

Domestic Unit. Marriage and the nuclear family have become the most common relationships in the middle economic strata. Salaried employment in the oil industry has enabled men to fulfill their roles as husbands and fathers. Women's roles changed after agriculture and domestic industry lost economic importance. Raising children and taking care of the household became their primary tasks. Monogamy and the nuclear family are still not as predominant as in the United States and Europe, however.

Inheritance. Inheritance rules vary on each island and between ethnic and socioeconomic groups.

Kin Groups. In the upper and middle classes, kinship rules are bilateral. In the matrifocal household type, kinship rules stress matrilinear descent.

Socialization

Infant Care. The mother takes care of the children. Grandmothers and older children assist in the care of younger children.

Child Rearing and Education. The educational system is based on the Dutch educational reforms of the 1960s. At age four, children attend kindergarten and, after age six, primary school. After age twelve, they enroll in secondary or vocational schools. Many students go to Holland for further studies.

Although Dutch is the language of only a small percentage of the population, it is the official language of instruction in most schools.

Higher Education. The Curaçao Teacher Training College and the University of the Netherlands Antilles, which has departments of law and technology, provide higher education. The university is located on Curaçao and Sint Maarten.

Etiquette

Formal etiquette is adapted from European etiquette. The small scale of the island societies influences everyday interaction patterns. To outside observers, communication styles lack openness and goal orientation. Respect for authority structures and gender and age roles are important. Refusing a request is considered impolite.

Religion

Religious Beliefs. Roman Catholicism is the prevalent religion on Curaçao (81 percent) and Bonaire (82 percent). Dutch Reformed Protestantism is the religion of the traditional white elite and recent

Dutch migrants who are less than 3 percent of the population. Jewish colonists who came to Curaçao in the sixteenth century account for less than 1 percent. On the Windward Islands Dutch Protestantism and Catholicism have had less influence, but Catholicism has become the religion of 56 percent of Sabans and 41 percent of the inhabitants of Sint Maarten. Methodism, Anglicanism, and Adventism are widespread on Statia. Fourteen percent of Sabans are Anglican. Conservative sects and the New Age movement are becoming more popular on all the islands.

Religious Practitioners. *Brua* holds a position similar to that of Obeah on Trinidad. Originating from the word "witch," brua is a mixture of non-Christian spiritual practices. Practitioners use amulets, magic waters, and fortune-telling. Montamentu is an ecstatic Afro-Caribbean religion that was introduced by migrants from Santo Domingo in the 1950s. Roman Catholic and African deities are revered.

Death and Afterlife. Opinions on death and afterlife are in accordance with Christian doctrine. Afro-Caribbean religions mix Christian and African beliefs.

Medicine and Health Care

All the islands have general hospitals and/or medical centers, at least one geriatric home, and a pharmacy. Many people use medical services in the United States, Venezuela, Columbia, and the Netherlands. Specialists and surgeons from the Netherlands visit the Elisabeth Hospital on Curaçao on a regular basis.

Secular Celebrations

The traditional harvest celebration is called seú (Curaçao) or simadan (Bonaire). A crowd of people carrying harvest products parade through the streets accompanied by music on traditional instruments. The fifth, fifteenth, and fiftieth birthdays are celebrated with ceremony and gifts. The Dutch queen's birthday is celebrated on 30 April, and Emancipation Day on 1 July. The Antillean national festival day occurs on 21 October. The French and Dutch sides of Sint Maarten celebrate the feast day of Saint Martin on 12 November.

The Arts and Humanities

Support for the Arts. Since 1969, the Papiamentu and Afro-Antillean cultural expressions have influenced art forms. The white Creole elite on Curaçao leans toward European cultural traditions. Slavery and the pre-industrial rural life are points of reference. Few artists, with the exception of musicians, make a living from their art.

Literature. Each island has a literary tradition. On Curaçao, authors publish in Papiamentu or Dutch. In the Windward Islands, Sint Maarten is the literary center.

Graphic Arts. The natural landscape is a source of inspiration to many graphic artists. Sculpture often expresses the African past and African physical types. Professional artists exhibit locally and abroad. Tourism provides a market for nonprofessional artists.

Performance Arts. Oratory and music are the historical foundations of the performance arts. Since 1969, this tradition has inspired many musicians and dance and theater companies. Tambú and tumba, which have African roots, are to Curaçao what calypso is to Trinidad. Slavery and the slave rebellion of 1795 are sources of inspiration.

The State of the Physical and Social Sciences

The Caribbean Maritime Biological Institute has done research in marine biology since 1955. Since 1980, scientific progress has been strongest in the fields of history and archeology, the study of Dutch and Papiamentu literature, linguistics, and architecture. The University of the Netherlands Antilles has incorporated the Archeological Anthropological Institute of the Netherlands Antilles. The Jacob Dekker Instituut was founded in the late 1990s. It focuses on African history and culture and the African heritage on the Antilles. Because of a lack of local funds, scientific research relies on Dutch finances and scholars. The fact that both the Dutch and Papiamentu languages have a limited public hampers contacts with scientists from the Caribbean region.

National cuisine of Netherlands Antilles

The Netherlands Antilles are characterized by an incredibly colorful cuisine. This diversity is due to the fact that the territory belonged to the Netherlands for a long time. European culture naturalized on the islands. It's reflected in many aspects, including local dishes. However, the indigenous population increasingly influences everyday life, so it is not surprising to see classic Dutch steaks and local fish balls on one table.

The basis of the national cuisine in the Antilles is, of course, seafood. The surrounding sea is incredibly rich, so most of the local dishes include shrimp, lobster, all kinds of deep-sea fish, shells and even algae. Servings are abundantly seasoned with vegetable oil. Vegetables are used as a side dish. Local chefs regularly come up with something new to continue the culinary development of the islands. Until recently, local people used meat rarely. Now, classic steaks are cooked more and more often. Caribbean spices help to create a truly amazing combination.

There are dozens of local treats. Still, there are the most noteworthy dishes that every guest of the islands should try. For example, barbecued snapper or barracuda, several different types of salted cod, grilled shells stuffed with cactus fruits, and a soup called sopi kama piska, which includes bananas and fish or meat. It is also worth mentioning the soup called sopi di piska based on fish and coconut milk. This amazing combination has an unusual taste. The dish is in high demand not only among locals but also among tourists. Another treat, which can be safely called national, is called keshi yena. This baked mixture includes cheese, raisins, tomatoes, olives, as well as beef, poultry or fish

Local people do not disregard traditional Dutch dishes, whether it is light-salted fish or cheeses. If we talk specifically about culinary masterpieces that include meat, we have to mention special pies called pastechi. The meat filling in them is combined with spices. That's the most popular local snack. In restaurants, you can always find a lamb or goat stewed with vegetables, a unique iguana soup, and even a well-done poultry. The last dish has an uncommon name for this place, galina. However, most of the menu is still occupied by dishes that may seem very unusual. These include pork tails stewed with papaya and rice.

The dish is most often served with green beans. Do not forget about the traditional everyday cuisine, which is simpler, but still remains unique. Bean pancakes, pea porridge, okra soup are served in almost any cafe. You can taste coconut or potato pudding, as well as a pie with guava as a dessert. However, remember that each of the islands has its own distinctive features, as well as its own name for a particular dish

A special attention should be paid to drinks. Alcoholic beverages are popular on the Antilles. The beer industry can even give odds to many other countries. The echo of the Dutch is still reflected in beer brands such as Heineken or Amstel, well known all over the world. Of course, when talking about the islands located in the Caribbean one should not forget about the upscale rum. Various liquors are produced both by natives, who sell these drinks, as well as large enterprises. There is the local brand, Saba-Spice, that produces a unique drink of rum, anise, cloves, nutmeg, and orange peel

Cultural Life

The three islands are quite different from each other and all have quite some special features compared to mainland European Netherlands. They differ not only in climate and culture, but also in administrative and legal provisions. However, being part of the

Kingdom of The Netherlands means stability and a sound legal and financial framework. These are small modern communities where local culture and traditions are firmly embedded in the society.

For Bonaire, St. Eustatius and Saba this means having a favorable business climate and that entrepreneurs and businesses follow a clear licensing procedure in order to be established and registered. The Bonaire Chamber of Commerce is strongly being modernized in different areas, while a new Chamber of Commerce was set up for Saba/St. Eustatius. Entrepreneurs may go to the Chamber for advice, guidance and coaching through a starters' plan of action that the Ministry of EZ has made possible in cooperation with the Chambers of Commerce.

The financial business instruments will be made available for applications from the Caribbean Netherlands, meaning that banks in the Caribbean Netherlands will be able to insure business loans (also micro loans) among others with the National Government in case of insufficient collateral.

The Ministry works with the governments and the tourist boards to assist Caribbean Netherlands with the marketing and promotion of the tourism potential. The Ministry of EZ supports the island governments and organizations in looking for ways to improve the services for the consumer in the postal, telecommunications, metrological and energy sectors. In addition, the Ministry encourages energy saving and the use of sustainable energy sources, such as wind and solar energy. Plans developed to this end in cooperation with the electricity companies on the islands are being implemented by way of concrete projects .

Both marine and terrestrial nature deserve the utmost care. Whether it is the 'Washington Slagbaai National Park' on Bonaire, the underwater atoll 'The Saba bank' near Saba or the National Park 'The Quill' on St. Eustatius. To protect marine life there is an integral nature conservation plan. Together with the Executive Councils, the conservation organizations, the National Forest Service in the Netherlands and the Ministries of Infrastructure and the Environment, the Ministry of EZ wants to actively and optimally provide this care for the islands. Furthermore, the Ministry of EZ wishes to encourage sustainable agriculture in the Caribbean Netherlands.

The pre-Lenten Carnival in February and the New Year's festivities are colourful celebrations. The Bonaire International Sailing Regatta is held every October, attracting boating enthusiasts from around the world. Many islanders also participate in martial arts, and football (soccer) and baseball are very popular. Saba, which is steep and tiny, has little flat land for athletic fields, but tennis courts there double as basketball and volleyball courts, and both men's and women's games are enthusiastically played. The islands first competed in the Olympics at the 1952 Summer Games in Helsinki.

There are a number of national parks, marine parks, and nature reserves on the islands. Notable among them are the Saba National Marine Park, which encircles the island and preserves and manages Saba's coral reef, and Christoffel Park on Curaçao, which covers 7 square miles (18 square km) and showcases the island's wide variety of natural flora and fauna. Several daily newspapers are published, in Dutch, English, and Papiamentu. There are also a number of local radio and television broadcast stations, and satellite television programming is available.

Food and Economy

Food in Daily Life. Traditional food customs differ between the islands, but all of them are variations of Caribbean Creole cuisine. Typical traditional foods are funchi, a maize porridge, and pan bati, a pancake made of maize flour. Funchi and pan bati combined with carni stoba (a goat stew) form the basis of the traditional meal. Bolo pretu (black cake) is prepared only for special occasions. Fast food and international cuisine have become more popular since the establishment of tourism.

Basic Economy. The economy centers on oil refining, ship repair, tourism, financial services, and the transit trade. Curaçao was a major center of offshore business but lost many clients after the United States and the Netherlands signed tax treaties in the 1980s. Efforts to stimulate tourism on Curaçao have been only partly successful. Market protection has resulted in the establishment of local industries for the production of soap and beer, but the effects have been limited to Curaçao. On Sint Maarten, tourism developed in the 1960s. Saba and Sint Eustatius depend on tourists from Sint Maarten. Bonairean tourism doubled between 1986 and 1995, and that island also has oil transshipment facilities. Underemployment climbed to 15 percent on Curaçao and 17 percent on Sint Maarten during the 1990s. Emigration by unemployed persons from the lower classes has caused social problems in the Netherlands.

Land Tenure and Property. There are three types of land tenure: regular landed property, hereditary tenure or long lease, and the renting of government land. For economic purposes, especially in the oil and tourism industries, government lands are rented in long renewable leases

Unlike most other Caribbean islands, the Netherlands Antilles seldom depended on the export of sugar or other plantation crops, which could not grow well in the dry climate of the larger islands. Instead, Curaçao (and during the 18th century Sint Eustatius) developed into a centre of regional trading and finance, activities that, together with oil refining and tourism, became the basis of the islands' economy. Willemstad in particular became an important Caribbean banking centre. Tourism and other services becameincreasingly important throughout the islands.

Agriculture, fishing, forestry, and mining play minor roles in the economy of the islands. Curaçao has some calcium phosphate mining; salt is processed on Bonaire. Sugarcane and cotton plantations were once established on Saint Martin and Sint Eustatius. Curaçao was at one time used mainly for livestock raising, but, after the overgrazing of land, new small-scale agricultural ventures were begun, such as the cultivation of aloes for pharmaceutical products and oranges for Curaçao liqueur. Aloes are also grown on Bonaire. Fish are important to the economy of Sint Maarten. Farmers on Saba raise livestock and cultivate vegetables, particularly potatoes, which are exported to neighbouring islands.

The main industry of Curaçao is oil refining, which started with the exploitation of Venezuelan oil fields in 1914 and the opening in 1918 of an oil refinery on Curaçao. Curaçao also produces liqueurs. Bonaire has a textile factory and Sint Maarten a rum distillery. Other factories produce electronic parts and cigarettes.

Curaçao refines and reexports a major portion of the oil extracted from Venezuelan territory, and petroleum and petroleum products are the island's main exports. The entrepôt trade in the free ports of Curaçao is also significant. Curaçao's foreign trade is mainly with Venezuela, the United States, the Netherlands, and several countries of Central America and the Caribbean. Most of the islands' requirements of food and commercial goods are met by imports.

The islands have extensive road systems. There are international airports at Curaçao, Bonaire, and Sint Maarten; Sint Eustatius and Saba also have airfields. Curaçao is a major point of shipping for the petroleum industry, and Sint Maarten is a leading Caribbean port of call for cruise ships.

History

The islands known as the Netherlands Antilles originally were inhabited by Arawak and Carib Indians; the arrival in the early 16th century of the Spanish caused the decimation of the native population. The Dutch, attracted by salt deposits, occupied the islands in the early 17th century, and, except for brief periods of British occupation, the islands have remained Dutch possessions. Through much of the 17th and 18th centuries, the islands prospered from Dutch trade in slaves, plantation products, and contraband, but the economy declined from 1816 until 1914.

Colonial rule

Curaçao
The first Europeans to sight Curaçao were Alonso de Ojeda and Amerigo Vespucci in 1499, and the area was settled in 1527 by the Spanish, who used it mainly for livestock raising. In 1634 Johannes van

Walbeeck of the Dutch West India Company occupied and fortified the island, which became the base for a rich entrepôt trade flourishing through the 18th century. During the colonial period, Curaçao was a major Caribbean centre for the transatlantic slave trade.

There were two short periods during the Napoleonic Wars when Curaçao was held by the British, but it was returned to the Netherlands by the Treaty of Paris in 1815. The 19th century was a period of economic decline partially alleviated by the cultivation of aloes and oranges. Only after the construction of the Schottegat oil refinery (opened in 1918), however, did economic conditions improve greatly.

Bonaire
Ojeda and Vespucci also sighted Bonaire during their voyage in 1499. The island was settled by the Spanish in 1501 and claimed by the Dutch in 1634. It became part of the Dutch West India Company in 1636 and remained a government plantation until 1863. From 1807 to 1814 it was under British control.

Sint Maarten
The island of Saint Martin was sighted by Christopher Columbus on Nov. 11, 1493 (St. Martin's Day), and was taken by French pirates in 1638. The Spanish settled there in 1640. In 1648 French and Dutch prisoners of war allegedly met after the Spanish departure and

amicably divided the island. The Dutch obtained Sint Maarten, the smaller but more valuable southern section, which contained large salt deposits.

Sint Eustatius
Sint Eustatius, first colonized by the French and English in 1625, was taken by the Dutch in 1632. It became the main centre of slave trade in the eastern Caribbean and by 1780 had a population of 2,500. In 1781 the British sacked Oranjestad, and the island never regained its trade. In the 17th and 18th centuries most of the land was under sugarcane cultivation.

Saba
Saba was settled by the Dutch in 1632 but, because of its inaccessibility and ruggedness, never achieved any economic importance.

Ethnic Relations. The Afro-Antillean past is a source of identity for most black Antilleans, but

different linguistic, historical, social, cultural, and racial backgrounds have strengthened insularism. To many people "yui di Korsow" (Child from Curaçao) refers only to Afro-Curaçaoans. White Creoles and Jewish Curaçaoans are symbolically excluded from the core population of Curaçao.

Urbanism, Architecture, and the Use of Space

Curaçao and Sint Maarten are the most densely populated and urbanized islands. Punda, the old center of Willemstad on Curaçao, has been on the United Nations World Heritage List since 1998. Plantation houses from the sixteenth to nineteenth centuries are spread over the island, next to the traditional *cunucu* houses in which poor whites, free blacks, and slaves used to live. Sint Maarten has residential areas on and between the many hillsides. The Bonairean cunucu house differs from the ones on Aruba and Curaçao in its ground plan. The cunucu house is built on a wooden frame and filled in with clay and grass. The roof is made of several layers of palm leaves. It consists minimally of one living room (*sala*), two bedrooms (*kamber*), and a kitchen, which is always situated downwind. The picturesque Saban cottage has style elements of traditional English cottages.

Political developments since World War II

After World War II, negotiations began with the aim of conferring a greater measure of self-government on the islands. On Dec. 15, 1954, the islands were made an autonomous part of the Netherlands. In 1969 Curaçao was torn by labour conflicts that led to riots and arson.

In the late 20th century, politics in the Netherlands Antilles were dominated by three issues: economic problems, the coming of independence, and the degree of autonomy to be afforded each island within the federation. By the mid-1970s it was clear that most of the Netherlands Antilles feared the economic consequences of independence. The Dutch government pressed for independence but insisted on preserving a federated structure embracing all the islands. In an unofficial referendum in 1977, Aruba voted to secede from the Antilles federation but remained within the kingdom; it formally achieved that status in 1986. By 1978 all the islands had accepted the concept of insular self-determination.

In 1989 the political leadership of Sint Maarten announced its desire to achieve full independence in the shortest possible term; secessionist feelings were fueled by animosity toward the central administration in Curaçao. An investigation by the government of the Netherlands into the administration of Sint Maarten resulted in 1993 in the arrest of two prominent leaders on charges of corruption and led to closer supervision by the metropolitan government of the island's affairs.

In 2006 the people of the islands agreed, along with the Dutch government, to dismantle the Netherlands Antilles, although none of the islands chose independence. On Oct. 10, 2010, St. Maarten and Curaçao became autonomous countries within the Netherlands, and Bonaire, Saba, and Sint Eustatius became special municipalities of the Netherlands.

Military Activity. Military camps on Curaçao and Aruba protect the islands and their territorial waters. The Coast Guard of the Netherlands Antilles and Aruba became operative in 1995 to protect the Netherlands Antilles and Aruba and their territorial waters from drug trafficking.

Social Welfare and Change Programs

There is a social welfare plan called the Social Safety Net on Curaçao, to which the Netherlands contributes financially. The results have been meager and the exodus of young unemployed Antilleans to the Netherlands has increased.

Nongovernmental Organizations and Other Associations

OKSNA (Body for Cultural Cooperation Netherlands Antilles) is a nongovernmental advisory board that advises the minister of culture on the allocation of subsidies from the Dutch development aid program for cultural and scientific projects. Centro pa Desaroyo di Antiyas (CEDE Antiyas) allocates funds to social and educational projects. OKSNA and CEDE Antiyas receive funds from the Dutch development aid program. Welfare organizations focus on areas ranging from day care centers to the care of the elderly. The government supports many of these activities

Government and Society

Prior to its dissolution in 2010, the Netherlands Antilles was a self-governing part of the Kingdom of the Netherlands. The head of state was the Dutch monarch, represented by a governor nominated by the local government and appointed by the crown. The head of government was a prime minister, who led a Council of Ministers. The council was responsible to the unicameral legislature (Staten), whose members were elected to four-year terms by universal adult suffrage. Beginning in 1992, education in the Netherlands Antilles was compulsory from age 6 to age 17, and the literacy rate was nearly on a par with that of the metropolitan Netherlands. Local authority was exercised by an Island Council, an Executive Council, and a lieutenant governor on each island.

Territories
Bonaire
Bonaire's history

Bonaire's history is deeply rooted in its inhabitants and their culture. The tranquil beauty of the island is reflected in the faces of her people. From the first inhabitants, the Caiquetios (a branch of the Arawak Indians) who sailed from the coast of Venezuela almost 1000 years ago, to the many cultures now living and working in Bonaire today, the island has a distinct character that is all its own.

Bonaire History The first Europeans came to Bonaire in 1499, when Alonso de Ojeda and Amerigo Vespucci arrived and claimed it for Spain. Finding little of commercial value and seeing no future for large-scale agriculture, the Spanish decided not to develop the island. Instead, they unceremoniously enslaved the Indians and moved them off to work in the plantations on the Island of Hispanolia, effectively leaving the island unpopulated.

The name Bonaire is thought to have originally come from the Caiquetio word 'Bonay', a name that meant low country. The early Spanish and Dutch modified its spelling to Bojnaj and also Bonaire. The French influence while present at various times never was strong enough to make the assumption that the name means 'good air'. Regardless of how the name came about, the island remained as a lonely outpost until 1526.

It was in that year, 1526, that cattle were brought to the island by then governor Juan de Ampues. Some of the Caiquetios were returned to act as laborers and in a few years, the island became a center for raising other animals such as sheep, goats, pigs, horses and donkeys. Since they were being raised more for their skins and not their meat, they required little tending and were allowed to roam and fend for themselves. The result was large herds of animals that far outnumbered the population. Today, there are a number of wild donkeys that still inhabit the Kunuku (outback) and many goats can also be seen foraging in less populated areas of the island.

Bonaire's early years were not ones of prosperity. Her inhabitants were mostly convicts from other Spanish Colonies in South America. The only permanent settlement was the village of Rincon, located far inland where it was thought to be safe from marauding pirates. In those years, development was discouraged in favor of the richer, more productive colonies.

In 1633, the Dutch took possession of Curacao, Bonaire and Aruba. The largest island, Curacao, emerged as a center of the notorious slave trade. Bonaire then became a plantation island belonging to the Dutch West Indies Company. It was during those early years that the first African slaves were forced to work, cutting dyewood and cultivating maize and harvesting solar salt. Grim reminders of those days still remain in the form of slave huts and salt pans which were laboriously constructed by hand. They are an important part of the island's heritage and have been left to stand mute testimony to Bonaire's repressive beginning.

Until 1816, ownership of Bonaire changed hands a number of times, finally being returned that year to the Dutch as a result of the Treaty of Paris. A small fort, Fort Oranje, was built to protect the island's main resource, salt. Salt was one commodity that Bonaire had in endless supply, although it took back breaking slave labor to produce it. In the early days of the industry, the most important use for salt was in the preservation of food, since refrigeration was still centuries away.

By 1837, Bonaire was a thriving center of salt production. The government, who by then controlled the industry, built four obelisks, each painted a different color, red, white, blue and orange (the colors of the Dutch Flag and the Royal House of Orange). They were erected strategically near areas of the salt lake. The idea was to signal ships where to pick up their cargoes of salt. A flag of the corresponding color was raised atop a flagpole, thus signalling the ship's captain where to drop anchor. Three of the obelisks can still be seen today.

The abolition of slavery in 1863 signaled an end to the era of exploitation of those first Bonaireans. It was almost a hundred years later that the salt industry was revitalized. Today it is a division of Cargill, Incorporated, one of the largest businesses in the world. It also was during this time that the island began to attract visitors.

Tourism was born when the island government constructed the first ship's pier in the harbor. It allowed cruise ships to tie up alongside the wharf and discharge passengers. It also made it easier to bring in goods and supplies for the island's residents. Hotels began to spring up and cater to the early visitors who enjoyed the tranquility of Bonaire. In 1943, the construction of a modern airport south of Kralendijk made it even easier for tourists to reach the island.

The history continues to be written. The people of Bonaire are part of the past and are proud of what they have accomplished on an island that was abandoned hundreds of years ago and deemed useless by the Spanish. As for the future, Bonaireans welcome progress but have made a conscious decision to take time out and step back and to look at how it will impact their island and their lives. They have learned to balance their growt with the environment.

Bonaire Government & Economy

The seat of the Netherlands Antilles government lies in Willemstad, Curacao. Bonaire and each of the other four islands within the association maintain control over internal affairs, but it is the central government based in Curacao that regulates police affairs, post, telecommunications, aviation, public health, and education, among others. The Netherlands Antilles government is based on a parliamentary democracy, and Parliament comprises a council of ministers and a prime minister. Bonaire, the second largets of all the Netherlands Antilles, comprises six distinct townships and villages. The island runs it's internal affairs through an elected legislative council, an advisory council, and executive council, comprising elected members of the island council. A lietenant governor, who is appointed by the queen, lives in Kralendijk and oversees local issues.

Economy Over the years, Bonaire has developed an economy based on tourism, oil transference, salt production, and some light industry such as apparel manufacture and rice processing. By far, the oldest surviving industry on the island lies in the salt. Salt pans cover 10% of Bonaire's surface, and the island produces 441,000 tons (400,000 metric tons) per year. The Akzo Nobel Salt Company moved onto the island in 1963, and today it produces nearly half a million tons of salt at it's solar processing center (meaning after the salt is harvested and washed, it's dried by the sun) at Pekelmeer, at the southern tip of the island. This is the only spot today where salt is commercially produced. The salt harvest in rough grades used mainly for industry and ice-melting, rather than astable salt.

While Aruba and Curacao benefitted from the discovery of large quantities of oil in Venezuela in the early 20TH century, Bonaire did not. However, in 1975, the Bonaire Petroleum Corporation (BOPEC) was established. You'll see it today, at the northern end of the island near Gotomeer. The plant does not refine petroleum, but is a transfer center, stroing petroleum for transfer from large tankers to smaller ones.

The largest industry on Bonaire today is tourism. The 70,000 tourists who visit the island each year, a small number by Caribbean standards but just about right for Bonaire, contribute not only to direct sales such as hotel rooms and diving operators, but to related industries such as food and restaurants, retail sales, and transportation.

Bonaire's Culture

The Bonairean culture is reflected in the faces of her people. Its origins are as varied as are the ethnic roots of the 15,000 plus residents. The real Bonairean culture is based on traditions that go back many generations and are chronicled in the songs and dances that are performed during holidays and festivals. It is also based on strong family ties and a general respect for nature and an understanding of an environment that originally was foreign to those first settlers and slaves that were forced to work the inhospitable, arid land.

Kids Those early days of slavery conditioned the people to be strong and to maintain a spirit that marks Bonaire and her people as extremely friendly and ready to smile when approached. Most of the people will raise a hand and wave to total strangers on the street. It was during this time that the spirit of the people began to develop and they made up songs, invented dances and began to sing in the old African Tradition. These songs and dances evolved into festivals and have survived to become an important part of life and culture on Bonaire.

The dances of the Simidan and the Bari are the best known. The traditional Waltz, Mazurka and the Polka and the local "Baile di Sinta" (ribbon dance) were performed as well as the Rumba, the Carioca and

Merengue which came from other islands. American Jazz also influenced the local traditions of song and dance. Along with an eclectic assortment of homemade musical instruments, those early performers set the stage for a rich, local tradition.

Tourism

Travel Guide

On an island with some of the world's most breathtaking coasts and coral reefs, it's no surprise that residents of Bonaire drive around with license plates proclaiming it's a "Diver's Paradise."

Tourists flock to the Caribbean island of Bonaire throughout the year to enjoy perfect diving and snorkeling conditions found along the coasts, in addition to the world-class windsurfing and boating opportunities. Inland, this Dutch municipality offers spectacular landscapes, which can be traversed on foot, horseback or bicycle. An impressive array of wildlife inhabits the area, including a large flamingo population and more than 190 species of birds.

Healthy portions of hospitality are served up around Bonaire, and despite its small size, a vast array of accommodation options can be found. Most of the hotels and guesthouses tend to be affiliated with diving schools and are fairly small, however, a number of high-end resorts have been springing up in recent years to cater to increasing numbers of tourists. The island is surprisingly renowned for its diverse cuisine, which is based on soups, stews and fish, in addition to Argentine, Italian and Chinese dishes. Most restaurants close for a few hours during the day for a siesta.

Although the island is world-famous for its spectacular diving and snorkeling, Bonaire has much more to offer. Day trips are popular and include excursions to the National Park, kayaking through the mangroves and land sailing on the world's longest track. There are also some enthralling walking tours, particularly in the quaint and historic towns of Rincon, the oldest village in Bonaire, and the capital, Kralendijk.

The most efficient way to traverse the island is on four wheels and it is possible to ship a car to Bonaire. However, it is much easier to rent one from the airport or your hotel. The island has also experienced a steady increase in its taxis over recent years, primarily due to Bonaire's growing popularity as a cruise port. An informal bus service, using vans, runs daily between the larger destinations, in addition to a few medium sized tour buses.

Things to Do

Bonaire is a perfect retreat for those looking to relax and soak up the natural wonders found on the island and surrounding coastline. The abundance of marine wildlife and spectacular coral reefs draw visitors from around the globe to the blue depths of the Caribbean. Onshore, flora, fauna and an endless array of birds make for some great walks, treks and bicycle rides and there are a number of tour operators on hand to help you get the most out of your stay on this beautiful island.

Many visitors base themselves in the capital city of Kralendijk, Bonaire's main gateway from where a plethora of diving, snorkeling and boat tours depart. In addition to marine activities, there are an abundance of things to pursue inland, including hiking, horseback riding and cycling through the rugged backdrop and brilliant scenery.

Diving is by far the biggest pull to this charming Caribbean island, and with more than 50 dive sites and unspoiled coral reefs it's obvious why. The calm and unique waters around Bonaire make it ideal for diving throughout the year and with an annual 'nature tag' it is possible to explore the marine park year-round. An endless number of dive operators are located throughout Bonaire, including Captain Don's Habitat and Great Adventures Bonaire.

Bonaire is also renowned for it ideal windsurfing conditions, particularly around Lac Bay. The large, protected bay with its steady winds and year-round sunshine make it one of the world's top destinations for novices and professionals alike. Bonaire Windsurf Place provides lessons and rents equipment.

One of the best ways to uncover the diverse wildlife and natural beauty is on a hiking tour. The dirt roads and goat trails scattered around Bonaire are ideal for scaling, especially in the Washington Slagbaai National Park, which also has the island's highest peak, Brandaris Hill. Tours can be arranged through various operators, such as Rincon-based Soldachi Tours.

Another great way to check out Bonaire's fascinating scenery is horseback riding. The island is home to two stables which offer a few scenic routes along the beach and the backroads, visiting small communities and getting a feel for life as an islander. Rancho-Washikemba, on Bonaire's eastern coast, offers lessons and tours.

If you fancy trying your luck on the tables, gambling while the sun sets overhead is a great way to pass the time. Divi Flamingo Casino is an easy-going venue that has Blackjack, Roulette and slot machines, and is the Caribbean's only barefoot casino open daily.

Bird watching is an extremely popular pastime on the island due to the wide range of species which call the area home. More than 190 different varieties are present, including the Amazon parrot, parakeets and Bonaire's most famous resident, the pink flamingo. A flamingo sanctuary is located on the island, but it is not open to the public. It is possible to catch a glimpse of these timid creatures on tours organized by Bonaire Dive & Adventure

Attractions

Languishing in the Caribbean Ocean not far from the coast of Venezuela, Bonaire has maintained an air of seclusion and visitors come here throughout the year to soak up the sunshine and sea. However, there is plenty to keep you entertained inland, with many interesting natural attractions, wildlife and cultural points of significance, namely the Bonaire Museum and Washington-Slagbaai National Park.

Washington-Slagbaai National Park

One Bonaire's top attractions, this national park covers almost 20 percent of the land, or 5,643 hectares to be exact. It is a magnificent place to discover the island's wildlife, from turtles to flamingos, and sublime landscapes, which include mangroves, sand dunes and forests. Launched in 1969, the park welcomes around 23,000 visitors every year and has an information desk close to the entrance to teach visitors about the heritage and culture of the island. Address: Malmok,

Bonaire   Phone: +599-788-9015

Website:http://www.washingtonparkbonaire.org/index.html

Bonaire Museum

Located on the outskirts of the Kralendijk, the Bonaire Museum is set in a charming 130-year old villa. Exhibits include local sculptures, art and pottery that offer insight into the lives and culture of the community. Some of the impressive displays include paintings by local artist Winifred Dania. The museum was the first of its kind and is still the largest on the island. It also focuses on the study of plantation house architecture, which can be seen throughout the island. Address: Kaya J Ree 7 Kralendijk Phone: +599-717-8868

The Grotto of Lourdes

In 1958, local resident Emma Pourier visited Lourdes, the France-based holy place of worship to commemorate the 100th anniversary since the supposed apparition of the Virgin Mary. Upon her return to Bonaire, she convinced the local priest to create a shrine on the island to spread and enhance the Catholic religion. A suitable cave was found near the town of Rincon and the grotto was constructed. Today, both locals and visitors can enjoy a trip to the shrine for a peaceful moment of reflection in front of the statue. Address: Rincon, Bonaire

The King's Storehouse

Bonaire's second oldest building, the *Mangazina di Rei*, or King's Storehouse was initially used to house a large quantity of the island's crops and largest export, salt. These days, the structure is slightly more glamorous, home to a botanical garden, museum and community center. The exhibits explore the anthropological and architectural history of the island and has numerous replicas of traditional stone houses which once formed Bonaire's townscape. Address: Rincon, Bonaire

Boka Onima
Folklore states that Boka Onima was the arrival point of the first man to Bonaire. A practically impossible destination on which to land due to the surrounding cliffs and sloping beaches, the inlet primarily draws crowds today because of the nearby rock drawings. The age of these primitive works is yet to be determined, but it is believed to be the creation of the Caiqueto Indians whose art has also been found in caves on the South American mainland. Address: East coast, Bonaire

Butterfly Garden
A tropical oasis of nature and tranquility nestled in Bonaire's beautiful flora, the Butterfly Garden exhibits a wide array of species native to the island and surrounding area, primarily Costa Rica. Located on the outskirts of Kralendijk, the farm is easily accessed from the capital and is open from Tuesday to Sunday. The Butterfly Garden is also home to

a highly-regarded restaurant which serves up some great dishes while you relax in the shaded garden around a pond brimming with koi fish. Address: Kaminda Lac 101, Kralendijk, Bonaire Website: http://www.butterflygardenbonaire.com/

Donkey Sanctuary
Formed in 1993 to look after the island's wounded and orphaned donkeys, the sanctuary now provides shelter to most of the population of Bonaire's donkeys. The sanctuary is home to more than 400 animals, which is always increasing. Many donkeys are rescued and treated, where they are able to live out their years in peace and any money raised goes back into the upkeep of the facility. There is also a placid garden where visitors can relax and admire the native iguanas and turtles, or look out over the salt planes to catch a glance of a flamingo. Address: Bonaire Phone: +599 95 607 607 Website: www.donkeysanctuary.com

Shopping and Leisure

While Bonaire is not particularly recognized as a great shopping destination, there are some great outlets with enticing and reasonably priced goods. Unlike many other Caribbean hotspots, the island is not littered with souvenir shops selling trinkets and the usual over-priced vacation gifts. There is one quirky shopping avenue in Kralendijk, featuring a variety of small, boutiques and unique merchants from Dutch cheese to Cuban cigars. Reasonably priced, high-quality china and gold jewelry can also be found on this stretch.

A number of shops within the resorts offer products and prices comparable to those back in the US and Europe. It is worth noting that Cuban cigars cannot be imported back to the US. A trip to the Bonaire arts and crafts market is also highly-recommended if you want to get a flavor of the local scene and purchase gifts to take home.

The original downtown buildings along Kaya Grandi date back to the late 1800's, traditionally housing families upstairs and shops below. Some of these have been renovated and restored, providing an air of authenticity and a charming atmosphere. If you are lucky enough to be in Bonaire on the first Saturday of the month, head over to Rincon Street Market and practice your haggling skills amongst the ramshackle collection of stalls.

There are also a few malls on the island, which cater to the everyday requirements of most travelers and are useful places to pick up clothes, toiletries and food. A number of stores, particularly in the open-air Harborside Mall, focus on equipment for diving, windsurfing and other marine activities, in addition to beachwear. High-end cosmetics and perfumers are also found in abundance, in addition to a wide assortment of liquors and wines. Reductions on duty-free imports make these products fairly cheap, but it is always advised to check how much you can bring back. Bear in mind it is illegal to take sea fans, coral and conch shells off the island.

Transportation

Bonaire Taxis and Car Rental

Taxis are the only form of public transportation on the island and are a fairly inexpensive way to explore Bonaire. Most drivers speak good English and are usually held to a high-standard. *Taxi 14 Kenneth and Katharina* (+599-700-3026) and *Taxi # 9 Christie Dovale* (+599-795-3456) are both well known local companies.

Car rental is available on the island and is a great way to get around, however, the driver must have a valid license from the US, Canada or Europe. Vehicles can be rented primarily from the airport and in downtown Kralendijk. Local firm, *Bonaire Rent a Car* (+599-786-6090) offers competitive rates and is a popular choice. Motorbikes and mopeds are also available for hire through *Rento Fun Drive* (+599-717-2408). The roads are clearly marked and driving is done on the right hand side of the road. Adhere to the speed limits because a donkey or goat in the middle of the road may surprise you.

Bonaire Water Taxis

Twice daily water taxis run between Bonaire and nearby Klein Bonaire, leaving from the main pier. Water taxi is the only way to reach this tiny island unless you rent a boat. The trip is an extremely pleasant experience and great daytrip with gentle music playing while you knock back a couple of cold ones en route.

Bonaire Boat Rental
Renting a private boat is a fantastic way to traverse the coastline of Bonaire and Klein Bonaire at you own leisure. They can be borrowed for half a day or full day through *Blue Bay Rentals* (+599-701-5500).

Airports
Flamingo International Airport

Situated close to Bonaire's capital, Flamingo International Airport is the third largest in the former Netherlands Antilles, receiving more than 21,000 passengers a year. The original airport opened in 1945 and was upgraded in the 1950's. In addition to a variety of connections to nearby islands, the airport has flights to a number of major European and North American cities, such as Miami and Amsterdam. The most popular airlines are local carriers Dutch Antilles Express and EZAir, for which Flamingo International is a hub, in addition to KLM, Delta Air Lines and United Airlines.

There's a range of dining options, bars and a recently updated departure hall, in addition to a few duty-free stores. Car rental through major international chains *Avis* and *Hertz*, and local firms is available, and there's always a number of taxis waiting outside. Further plans to upgrade the facility in coming years are in place to accommodate the growing tourist arrivals.

Queen Beatrix International Airport (Aruba)

The Netherlands Antilles largest airport, Queen Beatrix International Airport welcomed more than 1 million passengers in 2011. The one terminal facility has direct and connecting flights to various destinations worldwide. About 30 airlines fly from Aruba, the most active being United Airlines, Gol Transportes Aereos and Avior Airlines. In recent years, the busiest routes have been to New York, Miami and Newark. The terminal has a good selection of restaurants, fast-food chains, bars and duty-free stores. Transfers to Bonaire's Flamingo International are commonplace, and it is also possible to travel by sea. All major car rental companies are present at the airport, in addition to taxis and bus services.

Simon Bolivar International Airport of Maiquetia (Venezuela)

Located about 13 miles outside the capital city of Caracas, Simon Bolivar Airport is the main gateway to Venezuela with almost 10 million travelers passing through in 2011. Due to its proximity to the ABC Dutch Antilles, this airport is a popular option for long haul arrivals who find it more practical to connect from here to Bonaire in the Southern Caribbean. The airport has two terminals, both of which include a variety of duty-free stores, restaurants and bars. Major airlines flying from Caracas include Aserca Airlines, Conviasa and RUTACA Airlines.

Travel Tips

Language: Dutch is the official language of Bonaire and is spoken by almost everybody; however, the native language is Papiamentu. Spoken exclusively on the ABC islands (Aruba, Bonaire and Curacao), Papiamento is a mix of Dutch, Spanish, Portuguese, Caribbean and African tounges. English is also widely spoken around the island and at tourist attractions.

Currency: Since January 2011, Bonaire has used the US dollar ($) as its official currency, with US $1 divided into 100 cents, but the Netherlands Antilles Guilder (NAFI) is still accepted everywhere. Currency can be exchanged at banks, airport and some hotels. ATMs are widely available, particularly at banks and shopping malls. Major credit cards are accepted in some establishments, but it's always best to check for your card supplier's mark before trying to make a purchase. Travelers' checks can be exchanged at banks with proper proof of identity.

Time: The island is on Atlantic Standard Time, which is either three or four hours behind GMT (GMT -3/-4), depending on Daylight Saving Time.

Electricity: Bonaire uses electricity at 220V with Europlug and Schuko plug sockets. Visitors wishing to use electrical appliances that operate according to a different voltage in Bonaire will need a transformer, while appliances that have different plugs to the region's Type B plugs will need a plug adaptor. Most US appliances do not require an adaptor.

Communications: The dialing code for Bonaire is +599. Purchasing a SIM card is straightforward and major local networks are Digicel and CHIPPIE. Most of the island has mobile phone coverage. Internet cafes are rather infrequent outside of the capital city, although most resorts have wireless service, usually for a fee.

Duty-free: Duty-free alcohol, cosmetics, perfume and other items are available to international passengers at Flamingo International Airport. Customs allowances depend on the country you're entering, with passengers able to purchase up to 400 cigarettes, two liters of distilled beverages and two liters of wine from the duty-free store.

Tourist Office: Tourism Corporation Bonaire, Kralendijk: +599-717-8322 or www.tourismbonaire.com.

Consulates and Embassies in Bonaire: US Consulate, Curacao: +599-9461-3066 British Consulate, Curacao: +599-9461-3900 Honorary Consul of Canada, Curacao: +599-9466-1115 Australian Consulate, Santiago, Chile: +562-550-3500

Emergency: Ambulance: 114 Police: 911

Visas and Vaccinations

Citizens of the UK, Germany, Spain and several others do not require a visa to stay in Bonaire for up to 90 days, while residents of The Netherlands, Belgium and Luxembourg do not even need a passport to enter the country. Nationals of the US, Australia and Canada can stay on the island for up to two weeks without a visa. Passports must be valid for at least six months upon arrival. Travelers from other countries should check their visa requirements at http://www.infobonaire.com/entryrequirements.html.

Health and Safety

Very little crime is reported in Bonaire; however, the usual precautions are always worth keeping in mind. Try to avoid traveling alone at night and avoid carrying valuables or large amounts of money. There are few signs of poverty and locals tend to be extremely friendly. Attacks against tourists are almost unheard of; however, it always helps to keep an eye on belongings, especially in large crowds. Valuables should not be left unattended on the beach or in hotel rooms and always use the safety deposit box.

Tap water and the local food are both fine for consumption. It is always worth investing in private healthcare before visiting Bonaire as medical offices are not few and far between. The island's only hospital, the 60-bed Hospitaal San Francisco in Kralendijk, has comprehensive emergency facilities. Vaccinations are not necessary and Malaria and Yellow Fever are not an issue. If medication is required, pharmacies can found throughout the capital in some smaller communities, usually keeping standard hours.

Festivals and Events

Bonaire has a rich culture and as a result is home to many festivals throughout the year. One of the island's most celebrated gatherings is naturally Dive into Adventure, which incorporates numerous marine events. Music is also a pivotal part of the island's identity and every May Bonaire Heineken Jazz Festival comes to town, drawing many international visitors.

Bonaire Carnival

Late February/early March sees the most colorful and spectacular festival of the island's calendar and is one of the best times of the year to visit Bonaire. No matter where you go, it is virtually impossible to escape the party atmosphere and the beat of the Caribbean drum once it's in full-swing. The most elaborate and hedonistic celebrations tend occur on the streets of Kralendijk where everybody puts on crazy costumes and does away with their inhibitions. The dancing, drink and downright debauchery goes on for days with music, fireworks and huge parades.

Simadan Festival

A folk festival held in April, the celebration was originally a harvest event. Originally farmers, with the assistance of friends and family, would head to the fields to rake in the crop. It remains a family-orientated day with lavish feasts thrown, which tend to include signature dishes such as goat soup, *giambo* (okra soup) and *repa* (pancakes). The *wapa*, a traditional dance which involves rows of people moving simultaneously, is a highlight and sees most townsfolk join in.

Bonaire Dive Festival

Bonaire has hosted this dive festival every June since 1997, which focuses primarily on conservation. Non-profit organization CORAL (Coral Reef Alliance) hold the event annually in order to raise awareness of the preservation of marine beauty. The two-week event includes seminars, environmental awareness projects, underwater dives and cocktail parties.

Bonaire Heineken Jazz Festival

Held every July, Bonaire's jazz fest has been running since 2005. The main event takes place on Saturday night, while many other concerts and activities are held across the area. Each year, hundreds of visitors and established musicians head to the island for a number of workshops and interactive events help to promote jazz and music among the young population.

Bonaire International Sailing Regatta

An annual sailing event every October, the Bonaire regatta includes a variety of boat races along the coast. Vessels from around the world come to compete, while numerous windsurfing and freestyle competitions take place. After sunset, attention turns back to the shoreline, notably the Sea Promenade, Wilhelmina Park and Kralendijk, where jovial, usually booze-fueled, social events go on late into the evening.

Restaurants

Bonaire's finest Restaurants

The mixture of so many cultural backgrounds has combined to give a distinct flavor to the restaurants on Bonaire. The local eateries serve large, hearty portions at reasonable prices. They make lots of stoba (stews), sopi (soups) and hasa (fried) selections in addition to local specialties. The island also offers fine dining as well and you will be pleasantly surprised at the selection and high quality that our chefs create to tempt your palate. Don't worry about dressing up for dinner. Casual attire is welcomed everywhere and credit cards are accepted at most places. During busy seasons and weekends, it is best to make a reservation.

Calabas Restaurant

The Calabas Restaurant serves a casual beach-side buffet breakfast daily, offering both a light continental breakfast as well as a full American breakfast.

Tel: +(599) 717-8285

Fax: +(599) 717-8238

Chibi Chibi Restaurant and Bar

The Chibi Chibi Restaurant and bar- a colorful, romantic gathering spot-is open for lunch and dinner daily, and serves both traditional continental cuisine as well as fresh local seafood. Guests dining at the

Chibi Chibi are entertained by a multitude of tropical fish in the surf just below the restaurant.

Tel: +(599) 717-8285

Fax: +(599) 717-8238

KonTiki Beach Restaurant & Bar
A colorful, romantic place where you can enjoy international, reasonably priced food and drinks, inside in a cozy atmosphere or outside on the deck. From the shaded terrace you'll have a beautiful view over the bay. Open 7 days a week for breakfast, lunch and dinner.

Tel: +(599) 717-5369

Fax: +(599) 717-5368

La Balandra
La Balandra offers creative international specialties for Breakfast, Lunch, Cocktails and Dinner in a breathtaking seaside location. A private candlelight dinner on the beach may be arranged upon request and guarantees an unforgettable dining experience.

Tel: +(599) 717-7500

Rum Runners Restaurant
"Rum Runners" offers relaxed, oceanfront, open-air dining at renowned Captain Don's Habitat - friendly service, good food, attractive prices. Also featuring authentic Italian thin crust pizza

served at the "Pizza Temple" and great cocktails at the "Deco Stop Bar". "Rum Runners" is open 7 am to midnight - experience the ambiance only "Rum Runners" can offer.

Tel: +(599)717-8290

Fax: +(599) 717-2390

SAMUR Thai Dinner Sail
Sail into the sunset with the authentic Siamese junk SAMUR, built in Bangkok, Thailand, for a gourmet Thai dinner served on-board surrounded by oriental antiques and ambiance. Securely moored in our Marine Park at the most romantic location you will dine under the sparkling Caribbean night sky.

Tel: +(599) 717-5592

Fax: +(599) 786-5592

Travel Tips

Airport

Flamingo Airport has a runway of almost 1.5 miles (2.4 km) in length, long enough to accommodate 747 Jumbo Jets. The airport's designation is BON. (See also Departure Tax)

ATM / Banks

Bonaire has a number of banks, all of which have ATMs located conveniently around the island. Banking hours are Monday through

Friday 8 or 8:30am until 3:30 or 4pm. Many are opened during the lunch hour.

Currency

The Netherlands Antilles Guilder (NAFl.) is fixed at the exchange rate of 1.77 to the dollar for cash and 1.78 for traveler's cheques. Most stores and businesses exchange it at 1.75. You can spend dollars everywhere, but will likely receive your change in guilders. Traveler's checks and credit cards are widely accepted. Be sure to have your passport or positive ID when changing Traveler's cheques at banks.

Climate / Weather

The average air temperature is 82º Fahrenheit (30ºC) and 75% relative humidity. Average water temperature is 80ºF (29ºC). Rainfall averages 22" (52.8cm) per year. There is a constant trade wind that generally makes the evenings cool and comfortable. Average windspeed is 15 mph (25kph).

Customs

Besides articles for personal use, visitors over 15 are allowed 400 cigarettes, 50 cigars, 250 grams of tobacco, 2 liters of distillated beverages, 2 liters of wine.

Airport tax:

If your final destination is Curaçao, St. Maarten, St. Eustatius, Saba or

Aruba: US $6.- or ANG 10.- and a security tax of ANG 2.50. (*50 % discount for residents from 2 to 12 years and 60 years or older*) All other destinations: US $34,- or ANG 60.10. Children under 2 years old do not have to pay airport tax. You have to pay the airport tax before you check in your luggage.

Dress Code

Casual (but no beach wear) downtown. Evening clothes are casual to casual nice.

Drinking Age, Casino/Gambling and DRUG Laws

The legal drinking age on Bonaire is 18 for both beer and other alcohol. The legal age for gambling in a casino is 21.

The Netherlands Antilles has its own drug laws which are not the same as Holland. Our drug laws are not lenient.

Drinking water

The water is distilled from seawater and is perfectly safe to drink.

Driving License

Foreign and international licenses are accepted.

Electricity

127 volt, 50 cycle. 220 volt is also available at some resorts. Most U.S. appliances will work, however a bit hotter. Dive shops and resorts have stations for guest use for charging camera batteries, etc. It is recommended that you use them to avoid damage to delicate equipment.

Emergencies
Bonaire has the 60-bed hospital, Hospitaal San Francisco (Kaya Soeur Bartola #2, Kralendijk), and a number of doctors. There is an ambulance plane on call for emergencies. A hyperbaric recompression chamber is located adjacent to the hospital and is run by a highly trained staff - admittance via the emergency room at the hospital. The emergency phone number is 191.

Entry Requirements
US and Canadian citizens must have a valid Passport and a return or ongoing ticket. See our **entry requirements page** for more details.

Ferry Services
Many people ask about ferry services of any kind between Aruba, Curaçao, Bonaire, and Venezuela. There are no ferry services between Bonaire and Curacao or any other islands.
Travel between the islands is possible by air only, see our **air travel**

page.

Internet Access

Most of the accommodations offer (wireless) internet connections if you bring your own laptop with you. **Cyber City Internet Cafe** has 8 of the fastest computers with internet connection. Open from 09:00 AM till 21:00 PM, 7 days a week. However, there is also a 24 hour service by using our outdoor 'window' computers.

Language

Papiamentu (local language), Dutch, English and Spanish.

Store Hours

Most stores are open Monday through Saturday from between 8 or 9 AM until 12 noon when they close for one to two hours, then remain open until 6 PM. Hours vary widely and some stay open during lunch hour. The larger supermarkets are open from 8 AM until 8 PM (may close during lunch) and some may be open on Sundays from 11 AM to 2 PM.

Taxes, Tipping and Service Charges

There is a 5% tax on virtually all goods and services (NAOB tax). A room tax of US$6.50 is also charged per person per day. Car rental tax is US$3.50 per day.

Tipping is much the same as in the States. Some restaurants add a 10-15% service charge automatically, so if in doubt, ask.

Taxis - generally a 10% tip is greatly apppreciated. In dive shops, etc. 10% is also the norm.

Taxi

Taxis are available at the airport. From other locations you may call the taxi stand at the airport at Tel. 8100.

Telephone

Direct dialing is possible from most resorts. AT&T, MCI, etc. can also be accessed. The local telephone office, TELBO can also place calls to all locations. For on island calls, dial just the last four digits.

For cell phone users, you can rent a cellular phone for the length of your stay with Cell.Rent tel. 09-5692244 /6999, or CellularOne 790-8787. If you have a TDMA phone, CellularOne can also offer local service, contact them for details.

Time Zone

Atlantic Standard Time. Same time as the United States East Coast during Daylight Savings Time (mid-Spring to mid-Fall). Bonaire does not change time for Daylight Savings, as is the custom in the US and Europe.

Tourism Seasons

High Season Winter/Spring: Dec. 15 - Apr. 14

Low Season Summer/Fall: Apr. 15 - Dec. 14

Windy Season: May - Aug, moderate wind Jan-Apr

Rainy Season: Nov. - Jan.

Vaccinations

No vaccinations or preventative medications are recommended for travel to Bonaire. Yellow fever and Malaria are not a problem here. The Center for Disease Control in the the US offers updates and advisories for travellers.

Entry Requirements

Tourist entry is generally only for 14 days, but 30 days may be given. Extensions are available at immigration. EU passport holders may stay for up to 120 days, but must get an extension first from immigration. Tourists who apply for an extension beyond the 30 days must have travel insurance (medical & liability) for the duration of their extended stay.

Entry Requirements - Passport validity

You must hold a valid passport to enter Bonaire. Your passport must be valid for a minimum period of six months from the date of entry into Bonaire.

For further information on exactly what will be required at immigration please contact the Dutch Embassy or Consulate in your country.

Visas for the Caribbean parts of the Kingdom of the Netherlands

As of 10 October 2010 it is possible to visit more than one Caribbean part of the Kingdom of the Netherlands using a single visa. The visa is valid for all parts of the Kingdom of the Netherlands in the Caribbean for a visit as a tourist or for a short stay in the countries Aruba, Curaçao and St Maarten and for the Dutch Caribbean islands Bonaire, St Eustatius and Saba.

Visa exemption categories (Caribbean region)

The following categories are exempted from the visa requirement:

holders of a valid residence permit for the United States, Canada, the Schengen Area, the United Kingdom, Ireland or Switzerland;

- ✓ holders of a valid residence permit for the French part of St Maarten;
- ✓ holders of a valid residence permit for one of the countries or public bodies (Bonaire, St Eustatius and Saba) of the Kingdom of the Netherlands in the Caribbean;

Nationals of the countries listed below do not require a visa for the Caribbean part of the Kingdom of the Netherlands (the countries Aruba, Curaçao and Sint Maarten and the Dutch public bodies Bonaire, Sint Eustatius and Saba).

Andorra	Iceland
Antigua and Barbuda	Ireland
Argentina	Israel
Australia	Italy
Austria	Jamaica (visa IS required for Aruba and for St Maarten)
Bahamas	Japan
Barbados	Latvia
Belgium	Liechtenstein
Belize	Lithuania
Brazil	Luxembourg
Brunei	

Netherlands Antilles

Bulgaria	Macao: holders of Special Administrative Region passports
Canada	
Chile	Malaysia
Costa Rica	Malta
Croatia	Mauritius
Cyprus	Mexico
Czech Republic	Monaco
Denmark	New Zealand
Dominica	Nicaragua
Ecuador	Norway
El Salvador	Panama
Estonia	Paraguay
Finland	Poland
France	Portugal
Germany	Romania
Grenada	South Korea
Greece	Spain
Guatemala	St Kitts and Nevis
Guyana (visa IS required for St Maarten)	St Lucia
	St Vincent and the Grenadines

Honduras	Suriname
Hong Kong: holders of British National Overseas passports	Sweden
	Switzerland
Hong Kong: holders of Special Administrative Region passports	Taiwan
	Trinidad and Tobago
Hungary	United Kingdom
San Marino	United States of America
Seychelles	Uruguay
Singapore	Vatican City
Slovakia	Venezuela
Slovenia	

Some notes:

- ✓ The visa requirement applies to all children, regardless of age. They must have their own visa sticker, which means that they must have their own passport. Fees do not need to be paid for visa applications for children under the age of six.

- ✓ Even if married to a Dutch national, an alien whose nationality requires him or her to have a visa is still required to apply for a visa and pay the visa application fee.

Accommodation

Hotels

Bonaire Lodging - Hotels / Resorts - Apartments

Picture yourself enjoying the soothing, never ending sunshine of a Caribbean island, on a pink sandy beach, overlooking sparkling turquoise Caribbean waters, listening to the rustle of coconut palms and sipping on a Piña Colada.

Sounds like heaven, doesn't it? Well you're close. It's Bonaire. Tranquility such as this can also be found at numerous fine hotels / resorts on Bonaire. Most hotels have complete water sports facilities, sailing charters, activities, swimming pools, restaurants, car rentals, gift shops, airconditioning, telephone and television. Depending on your needs, apartment unit with kitchenettes and villas are available upon request..

Hotels and Resorts

Plaza Resort Bonaire

Plaza Resort Bonaire, the resort that has it all!

The Plaza Resort Bonaire is ideally located, enjoying one of Bonaire's small collection of white sand beaches, looking out over lagoons, a small harbour and the Caribbean Sea.

The Plaza's accommodation comes in a variety of spacious suites and villas. All have generously sized bedroom

s and bathrooms with all the modern facilities you would expect from a luxury resort.

Phone: +(599) - 717 2500

Fax: +(599) - 717 7133

E-mail: reservations@plazaresortbonaire.com

Blue Divers Bonaire

Blue Divers is a friendly and personal resort. The resort is very centrally located, within walking distance to the center of town, many restaurants and only about a minute walk from the ocean! All 10 apartments are self contained with kitchen and bathroom and surround a tropical, private courtyard with pool and sun deck.

Address: Kaya Norwega 1

Phone: +(599) 717-6860

Fax: +(599) 717-6865

E-mail: info@bluedivers-bonaire.com

Captain Don's Habitat

Whenever the whim... Oh, imagine the feeling: it's another perfect day, the aqua blue water is right in front of you calling relax, enjoy, experience the wonders of the tropical sea. Who cares what time of day it is, you grab your equipment from the dockside locker, step off the dock, and you're already soothed by warm, clear waters and delighted by schools of colorful fish.

Phone: +(599) 717 8290

Fax: +(599) 717 8240

E-mail: info@habitatbonaire.com

Divi Flamingo Beach Resort & Casino
The Divi Flamingo Beach Resort & Casino overlooks the turquoise Caribbean Sea. Intimate and informal, guests are invited to enjoy the comfortable 129 rooms and studios, all air-conditioned, with a private patio or balcony, two swimming pools and its own natural beach.

Phone: +(599) 717 8285

Fax: +(599) 717 8238

E-mail: info@divibonaire.com

Harbour Village Beach Club
Located within an exclusive beachfront residential enclave on the leeward side of the island of Bonaire, Harbour Village Beach Club offers incomparable serenity in a luxury retreat setting. The Club provides a peaceful elegance and the ultimate in seclusion.

An array of activities await guests of Harbour Village Beach Club including newly remodeled, elegantly appointed rooms and suites, an attentive staff and Club concierge. Guests have access to the club's amenities including its private white sand beach, dive and water sports center, beachfront restaurant, sun deck and pool, fitness center, spa services, tennis center, marina, meeting and conference facilities.

Phone: +(599) 717 7500

Fax: +(599) 717 7507

E-mail: reservationsusa@harbourvillage.com

KonTiki Beach Bonaire
KonTiki Beach Bonaire is located at Lac Bay Lagoon, a protected nature reserve. After a ten minute-drive from Kralendijk and the airport, you will
find KonTiki, a quiet, romantic place where you can enjoy good food and cool
drinks - either inside in a cosy atmosphere or outside on the deck. From the
shaded terrace you will have a beautiful view over the bay with its amazing
blue and green colours. With 18 apartments and one villa, KonTiki accommodates 50 guests in an intimate, quiet and unique setting. Owners
Martin & Miriam will do their utmost to serve their guests in every possible
way. The restaurant is open 7 days a week for breakfast, lunch and dinner.

Windsurf and dive packages with car rental can be arranged as well.

Phone: +(599) 717 5369

Fax: +(599) 717 5368

E-mail: info@kontikibonaire.com

Port Bonaire
The first to welcome you...and the last to bid farewell. The captivating colors of the ocean are steps away from your porch or balcony at Port Bonaire, an oceanside complex with 26 luxury 1, 2 and 3 bedroom apartments positioned around a swimming pool with gorgeous views of the ocean, coastline and Klein Bonaire. A tropical garden leads you to the shore line where the ocean invites you to explore the coral fronted waters, just a few fin kicks from this exclusive hideaway

Phone: +(599) - 717 2450

Fax: +(599) - 717 2459

E-mail: info@portbonaire.com

Bonaire Intimate Hotels and Resorts (Guesthouses, B&B)
Villa Safir Bonaire
The Villa guarantees you a great ocean view, and you can enjoy this view even from your room. The uphill location also guarantees a nice refreshing breeze. Our 3 guestrooms open into the porch where the fresh water swimming-pool is. This is also the place where you can enjoy your custom made breakfast. Each rooms has a comfortable

king-size bed, air-conditioning and also a ceiling fan. They all have a private bathroom/toilet

Phone: +(599) - 717 6564

E-mail: stay@villasafir.com

Website: www.villasafir.com

A small, intimate, primitive guest-house where a "personal touch" is our service style. So tell us how you would spend your ideal vacation, and we will do our utmost to make it a reality. The accommodations are set in a quiet residential location with stunning views over the Island and the Caribbean Sea. On a very clear day, you may even see Curacao and Aruba!

Address: Kaya Turkesa 7

Phone: +(599) - 795 6582

Fax: +(599) - 717 6584

E-mail: info@lapuravista.com

Weather

Weather & Climate - Temperature Averages

Bonaire is blessed with one of the gentlest climates in the Caribbean, with very little rainfall (less than 22 inches annually) and a prevailing easterly trade wind that provides a constistent 15 mph (= 25 Kmh) breeze. This trade wind is also one of the coral reefs best friends and a major reason these reefs are among the most prolific in the world. When the wind blows constinuously from the same direction, one side of the island has "rough" water conditions (the windward side), the other side (the leeside) is almost always clam. Since Bonaire lies at a 90 degree angle to its trade winds, the island's western side (where you'll find all of the snorkeling operations) is always calm and protected.

Not only does this provide perfect snorkeling conditions about 99% (no exaggeration) of the time, it also alows corals to grow prolifically in shallow water (rough water tends to knock some of the corals over, preventing them from attaining full growth). The low rainfall on Bonaire is also a blessing, since fresh water from rivers (there are no rivers on Bonaire) and rain runoff are enemies of the coral reef. Freshwater runoff almost contains sediments, which can harm the coral by literally smothering it.

Temperature Table											
	Average high		Average low		Warmest ever		Coldest ever		Average dew point		Average precipitation
Month	F	C	F	C	F	C	F	C	F	C	
January	84	28,9	76	24,4	89	31,2	70	21,1	72	22,2	2.1
February	85	29,4	76	24,4	95	35	68	20	72	22,2	1.1

March	86	30	77	25	90	32,2	70	21,1	72	22,2	0.7
April	87	30,6	78	25,6	93	33,9	72	22,2	74	23,3	0.9
May	88	31,1	79	26,1	95	35	72	22,2	75	23,8	0.8
June	88	31,1	80	26,7	100	37,8	68	20	75	23,8	0.8
July	89	31,7	79	26,1	102	38,9	68	20	75	23,9	1.3
August	89	31,7	80	26,7	99	37,2	68	20	75	23,8	1.7
September	89	31,7	80	26,7	100	37,8	72	22,2	76	24,4	1.7
October	88	31,1	79	26,1	97	36,1	73	22,8	76	24,4	3.2
November	87	30,6	79	26,1	96	35,6	68	20	75	23,9	3.6
December	85	29,4	77	25	91	32,8	68	20	73	22,8	3.7

Curacao

History of Curaçao

In many ways, Curaçao is the historical nexus of the Netherlands Antilles. The island, with its large and protected natural port, was charted before the 16th century and eventually became a major center for mercantile commerce. It is the birthplace of Papiamentu (as it is spelled on Curaçao), the polyglot lingua franca of the ABC Islands which is spoken to an extent as far north as the Netherlands Antilles islands of Sint Eustatius, Saba, and Sint Maarten. And the island is, on another level, the birthplace of the famous liqueur, Curaçao, perhaps more well known in some circles than the island itself.

The history of Curaçao begins with *Amerindian Arawaks*. The Arawaks and their subgroups migrated from regions of South America some 6,000 years ago, settling on various islands the discovered as they embarked on a centuries-long northward trek. The group that ended up in Curaçao were the *Caiquetios*, who gave the island it's name.

After the late-15th-century voyages of *Christopher Columbus* put the *Caribbean*, literally, on the maps, the area was wide open for European exploration. The Spanish soldier and explorer *Alonso de Ojeda*, joined by the Italian *Amerigo Vespucci*, set out on a voyage (1499 - 1500) to chart much of the South American coast and, in turn, several offshore islands in the area. One was Curaçao. As an aside, disputed claims are par for the course when it comes to Vespucci. One of many stories has it that during his voyage with de Ojeda, a number of sailors on his ship came down with scurvy, whereupon he dropped off the hapless souls on Curaçao on his way to South America.

On his return, he found the sailors alive and happy-presumably cured by the abundance of Vitamin C-laden fruit on the island. He then is said to have named the island Curaçao, after an archaic Portuguese word for "cure". Of course, Vespucci was Italian, not Portuguese, and de Ojeda was Spanish, but these stories seem to take on a life of their own, and are often much more fun than the real story. A more convincing theory is that the Spaniards called the island *Curazon*, for "*heart*", and the mapmakers of the day converted the spelling to the Portuguese Curaçao.

At any rate, soon after de Ojeda's voyage, the Spanish came in larger numbers. By the early 16th century they had pretty well determined that the island had little gold and not enough of a fresh water supply to establish large farms, and they abandoned it. Finally, the *Dutch West India Company*, a quasi-private, government-backed company, laid claim in 1634. The company installed the Dutch explorer *Peter Stuyvesant* as governor in 1642, and he soon established plantations on the island, each with its famous landhuizen-structures that can still be seen today. The plantations foundered in various forms of agriculture, but some were successful in growing peanuts, maize, and fruits. They soon found their niche in the production of salt, dried from the island's saline ponds. Within a few years after establishing the farming industry and some form of rule on Curaçao, Stuyvesant moved on to bigger shores.

With its deep port and protected shores, and with the establishment of several large forts, Curaçao soon became a safe place for the Dutch West India Company to conduct commerce. Chief among its endeavors was the trade of slaves from Africa, who then went on to the other islands of the Dutch West Indies and to the Spanish Main. It was during the slave trade days that *the language Papiamentu* began to form. The language, a mixture of Portuguese, Spanish, Dutch, and African dialects, became the main form of communication between slaves and their captors.

Also during this time, Jewish families from *Amsterdam* established settlements on Curaçao and attracted others from Europe and South America, fleeing from the remnants of the Spanish and Portuguese Inquisitions. By the early 18th century, the Jewish population in Curaçao had reached 2,000. In 1732, the community established the *Mikve Israel Emanuel Synagogue* in *Willemstad*, a structure that stands today. It is one of the oldest synagogues in the *Western Hemisphere* still in use.

During the early 18th century, the island's deep port and strategic position attracted the British and French, who as always were busy in the Caribbean, fighting over various islands in desperate struggles to control the profitable trade routes and sugar plantations of the larger islands. Brittain tossed out the Dutch twice, from 1800 to 1803, and again from 1807 to 1815. *The 1815 Treaty of Paris* settled a lot of disputes in the Caribbean, and it gave Curaçao back to the Dutch West India Company. Soon after the Dutch retook the island, it languished for a century. Slavery disappeared, and social and economic conditions were harsh.

In 1920, oil was discovered off the Venezuelan coast. This signaled a new era for Curaçao, and for its sister island in the ABCs, Aruba. The two islands became centers for distilling crude oil imported from

Venezuela, and Curaçao's *Royal Dutch Shell Refinery* became the island's biggest business and employer. Immigrants headed for Curaçao, many from other Caribbean nations, South America, and as far away as Asia. During WW II, the Allies judged Curaçao and its refinery to be important enough, and strategic enough, to establish an American military base at *Waterfort Arches*, near Willemstad.

After WW II, Curaçao joined the rest of the Caribbean in a loud clamor for independence. What it got instead was a measure of autonomy as an entity within the *Kingdom of the Netherlands*. Curaçao, along with, *Bonaire*, *Saba*, *Sint Eustatius*, and *Sint Maarten*, became the *Netherlands Antilles*, with the administrative center in Willemstad. Aruba separated from the other five islands on January 1, 1986. Sint Maarten and Curacao became independed on October 10, 2010 and the islands of Bonaire, Saba and Sint Eustatius became special municipalities within the country of the Netherlands.

Economy & Government
Government
Per October 10, 2012 Curaçao is an autonomous country within the Kingdom of the Netherlands. The locals have Dutch nationality and carry Dutch European Union passports.

The form of government is a parliamentary democracy, based on underlying premises such as freedom of association, the right to form political parties, freedom of the press, and freedom of speech.

Curaçao has two levels of government-a central (federal) and an insular (territorial) level.

The *Central Government's jurisdiction* covers mostly state affairs (legislation) and includes police, communications, taxation, public health, education, economic control, the establishment of enterprises, labor legislation, money and banking, and foreign currency.

The *Island Government* is responsible for the island territory affairs; it manages its own territorial affairs and has the power to enact laws. The island government is responsible for the infrastructure, harbors, airport, etc.

Economy

In modern times, Curaçao has expanded its infrastructure and modernized. The refinery is still big business, and now a large desalinization plant provides the island's potable water. The capital *Willemstad* has grown as well, and in the post-WW II period, the city experienced tremendous growth. In addition to other changes, bridges were added to provide easy access between the two downtown sections of the city, *Punda* and *Otrobanda*, which are separated by the *Sint Annabaai* (*St. Anna Bay*) channel.

Revenues on the island are dependent services and family transfers from The Netherlands, oil refinery earnings (representing more than 90% of all exports), offshore banking, and tourism. Curaçao's tourism is still growing, but it is that aspect of the island that makes it so appealing to many.

Travel and Tourism

Travel Guide

The 'C' of the ABC Netherlands Antilles group in the southern Caribbean, Curaçao (pronounced *cure-a-sow*) is a popular year-round destination for sun-seekers. It doesn't have the best beaches in the Caribbean, but the island's great weather, superb scuba diving, and Dutch charm are reason enough to visit.

Curaçao has many things going for it, not least its beaches, which are close to the main town and on the properties of many big hotels and resorts. Water sports are low-key, although there is excellent windsurfing and diving, and you can snorkel over the reefs. The beaches are good for families, couples and singletons, with quiet ones in the north.

Chief of sightseeing is the pleasant capital, Willemstad, which is best known for its low-rise skyline of colorful harbor front buildings. There is a popular floating market, along with an antique floating bridge and several forts. Willemstad can mostly be seen on foot and is within walking distance from the main beaches of Mambo and Kontiki.

Curaçao has good hotels, most being mid-range to high-end and residing on or near a beach. They typically come with good restaurants and lively entertainment, and sometimes spas and casinos for entertainment. The diverse culture has taught the island a great compliment of cuisines, while the nightlife is the busiest in this part of the Caribbean.

The shopping is intriguing and consists of an entire duty-free section tailored to the thousands of visiting cruise passengers, along with rows of boutiques and souvenirs shops for clothing and crafts. Value wise, Curaçao is on par with Aruba and Bonaire for eating out, shopping and accommodation, but you get slightly more for your money here than in the Bahamas.

Boat trips around the island are popular, from deep-sea fishing charters to cruises to nearby Klein. Aruba and Bonaire are also within reach by boat or 30-minute shuttle flight, while Curaçao itself has plenty to entice those with itchy feet. Christoffel National Park is a sizeable, hilly region of the north with hiking and caves, plus the island has good horseback riding potential.

Direct flights come in from around the Caribbean region and the US, Canada, Europe and South America. Major cruises also call on Willemstad. While not large, Curaçao doesn't have the most comprehensive transport network. Most tourists rely on taxis and buses for getting around, while car rental is reasonably priced and the driving relaxed.

Things to Do

Curaçao is surrounded by warm water and has many beaches near the capital of Willemstad providing plenty of things to do. Some of them offer water sports, including wakeboarding and sea kayaking, while the accessibility of coral reefs and wrecks along with clear water and reasonable prices make scuba diving particularly attractive.

Boat excursions run direct from the harbor in Willemstad aboard modern vessels or authentic clipper ships. Some operators also feature fishing excursions, although prices are steep and stocks limited. Most activities are accessible and easy to get to for the average tourist, as Curaçao is not large.

Curaçao scuba diving is some of the best in the region, with warm, clear water year round, good visibility, and lots of enticing things to see under the waves, including extensive sponges and sea anemones. Much of the coast is protected, including the huge Curaçao Underwater Marine Park in the south and Banda Abou National Park in the north. *Ocean Encounters* offers trips to the east coast to see the wreck of the *Superior Producer* and to the west for the Watamula and Mushroom Forest. *Diveversity Blue Bay* is perhaps the best operator for PADI courses if you're looking to get certified.

Curaçao has more than three dozen beaches, from popular family escapes with calm water for swimming near Willemstad, to secluded coves for a romantic getaway in the north. The south has the best beaches, while the north coast is rockier and less accessible. One of the most popular beaches is Mambo Beach, just east of Willemstad and good for bathing, swimming, and nightlife. It is also known as Seaquarium Beach for the popular Curaçao Aquarium. Blauwbaai, to the north of Willemstad, has better swimming conditions, while Daaibooi (south) is less touristy and great for snorkeling. Westpunt, in the north, also has good beaches, including Playa Kalki and nearby Playa Lagun.

Boat excursions often include sightseeing, lunch, and a snorkel, and may take in nearby islands. The *Bounty* is a favorite, running Wednesday, Friday, and Sunday from Sarifundy Marina. Tours are operated by *Bounty Adventures*, who also operates a catamaran to nearby Klein Curaçao Island. For sailing rigger style, try the *Insulinde*, which goes from Handelskade (next to Queen Emma Bridge) and includes a full day of activities. Prices are reasonable for a day on the water.

The fishing is not as good here as perhaps some of the other popular Caribbean destinations on account of limited stock through overfishing. However, if you have deep pockets, the continental shelf is nearby and deep-sea fishing charters head here daily. Be prepared to spend a lot though for a full or half-day trip. You can also fish nearer to the shore with the likes of *Let's Fish*, who operates 'catch and release' trips.

Exploring caves is a favorite pastime on Curaçao. The coral and limestone Hato Caves in the north of the island are especially impressive, carved out under the sea. They are located near the airport and tours run regularly from Willemstad. Highlights include stalactites, stalagmites, a waterfall and fruit bats. The caves in

Christoffel National Park in the northwest are noted for their Arawak paintings

Attractions

Not loaded with attractions, Curaçao still has enticing options for all types of visitor. The beaches are the main draw and can be found near to the capital, as well as in more secluded areas of the island, with Mambo Beach being the de facto day/night spot. The capital city itself is a hit, home to multicolored houses, harbor front forts, and a floating bridge. Getting around downtown is best done on foot, while buses and car rental are options for seeing more of the island.

Willemstad

Curaçao's capital is a central focus of the island with everything built up around it. It resides on a pretty harbor and is noted for its waterfront houses and interesting shopping areas. Amsterdam Fort sits at the mouth of the harbor and is a major landmark, while the Floating Market and Queen Emma Bridge are also worth checking out. For the best views of the town, harbor, and sea, head for the towering Queen Juliana Bridge (by car), which links the east and west sides of the marina mouth. Address: Willemstad, South CuraçaoPhone: n/a Website: n/a

Mambo Beach

This beach, noted both for its white sands, protected waters, facilities, and nightlife, is Curaçao's most popular. Also known as Seaquarium Beach—with the Curaçao Sea Aquarium at its southern end—Mambo is dotted with palm trees and umbrellas, and the water here is nice and shallow. It is backed by several big hotels and resorts, including the Curaçao Resort Spa & Casino and the Kontiki Dive & Beach Resort, which also fronts onto nearby Kontiki Beach. Both get crowded so get up early if you want to secure a prime sunbathing spot. Address: Bapor Kibra zone, Willemstad Phone: n/a Website: n/a

Christoffel National Park
Curaçao's largest protected region sits in the north and presides over lofty landscapes, a rich variety of flora and fauna, and Indian caves. Many plants and animals here cannot be found anywhere else on the island, including white tailed deer and wild orchids. Hiking trails are strewn across the area from easy strolling to a more intense hike up Mount Christoffel (recommended to do in early morning to avoid the heat). You can also drive there, but it pays to rent a car as the park is 40 minutes' from Willemstad. The park is open daily and has a reasonable entry fee. Address: Banda Abou, North Curaçao Phone: +599-9-864-0363 Website:http://www.christoffelpark.org/

Queen Emma Bridge

The 548-foot long 'Swinging Old Lady' is an old floating pontoon bridge that link the Point (Punda) and Other Side (Otrobanda) at the harbor mouth in Willemstad. The pedestrian-only walkway hails from the 1880's and is continually open and closing to allow boats passage. If the bridge needs to be up for a while, a ferry service is available between the two points. It's worth standing around to catch the bridge in action, with the Punda end powered, opened and hinged at the Otrobanda end. Address: St. Annabaai Channel, Willemstad Phone:n/a Website: n/a

Curaçao Ostrich Farm
Located on the northern side of the island, Curaçao Ostrich Farm makes a fun attraction for all. It's quite large and visitors can walk through the ostrich pens and feed or ride the birds. You get to see everything from chicks to full grown birds on an open-sided safari tour, which leaves hourly from the Zambezi restaurant. The restaurant is noted for its Afrikaans menu, while also on site are souvenirs at the Art of Africa shop. The Ostrich Farm is open every day and is only about a 20 minute drive from Willemstad. Address: St. Joris zone, Santa Catharin Phone: +599-9-747-2777 Website: http://www.ostrichfarm.net/

Curaçao Sea Aquarium

Definitely one for the kids is this fun aquarium with dolphin show. It features the vaunted Dolphin Academy and, due to its proximity to Willemstad (just south) and the beach, is one of the go-to attractions for families rain or shine. The aquarium employs an open-water-system—pumping fresh seawater through—and comes with giant turtles and presentations. If you want to swim with the dolphins, be sure to book well in advance. When you're done, the nearby Seaquarium Beach (also known as Mambo Beach) has many bars and eateries. Address: Bapor Kibra zone, Willemstad Phone: +599-9-461-6666 Website: http://Curaçao-sea-aquarium.com/en/index.html

Lagun Beach
Playa Lagun, one of Curaçao's more secluded bays, sits in the northwest of the island within the town of Lagun. The small bay is hemmed in by cliffs and has plenty of sand and a gentle slope, so it is a decent alternative to the busier shores near the capital. The snorkeling here is particularly good, with lots of marine life plus the Discover Diving Curaçao shop. Lagun Beach is about a 30-minute drive from Willemstad, but buses also run this route. Nearby is Christoffel National Park. Address: Lagun, Northwest Curaçao

Fort Amsterdam
A major landmark in Curaçao for many years, Fort Amsterdam resides at Willemstad harbor (on the Punda, south side). The former site of

the Netherlands Antilles' seat has the Governor's Palace, shops and eateries. It is photogenic and worth an hour or two of exploration. Across the water is the touristy Rif Fort while at the other end of the channel is Fort Nassau, on a hill. Address: Plaza Piar, Willemstad

Food and Restaurants

Food and restaurants in Curaçao are quite low-key and easy going compared to other higher profile Caribbean destinations. You can get about Willemstad, the capital, on foot to take in its eateries and bars, and there are options right in the city and at the beaches nearby. Other areas have less choice, with hotels typically providing all the entertainment. Along with bars and clubs are casinos and dancing under the night sky.

Bars and Pubbing in Curaçao

While Curaçao doesn't have the best nightlife in the Caribbean, it is one-up from nearby Aruba, and there are many places to let your hair down. Willemstad has the best of it, in particular within the Salina district, which is to the east of the town proper, backing the main beaches.

Head for Penstraat, which has many watering holes, including Blues (Avila Beach Hotel, Penstraat 130-134, Willemstad) known for its jazz and food. Mambo Beach is also fun at night and includes the *Wet & Wild Beach Club* (Seaquarium Beach, Bapor Kibra, Willemstad). It has free barbecue on Friday nights and a DJ and live music on Saturdays (to 1:30 a.m.).

There are several other night spots in the area, although they don't all go off in equal measure every night. Each place has its 'unofficial' night, which is fostered by the owners—see the *K-Pasa* (http://www.k-pasa.com/) tourism guide for more information. For a schooner of Amstel with the locals, take a look at the *Grand Café de Heeren* (Zuikertuintjeweg, Bloempot, Willemstad).

Curaçao also has many casinos in its plush resorts and these venues are a source of nightly entertainment. They typically have restaurants, bars, clubs, and live music, and include the *Carnaval Casino* (Renaissance Curaçao Resort, Baden Powelweg 1, Willemstad). Casinos often stay open until 4:00 a.m., while bars in general typically close around midnight or 1:00 a.m.

Dining and Cuisine in Curaçao

All main beaches have cafés and restaurants, with the best eating in Willemstad. Head to either side of the channel for a variety of choices, though the Point (Punda) has more options than the Other Side (Otrabanda). The Point on the east is where Willemstad proper, made up of multicolored houses, forts, and markets, is located. Dine on typical Dutch and European foods, Caribbean fare, and great seafood. Gouda cheese is very popular here.

There are many mouth-watering eateries in this area of Curaçao, including the *Plasa Bieu* (Punda, Willemstad), which has well-priced regional fare and is near the Old Market and floating bridge. The Pietermaai area of Punda (just east of the fort) also has good restaurants, including the *Eetcafe Old Dutch*(Pietermaai 25, Punda, Willemstad), a traditional brown café with Dutch food. On the Other Side is the highly rated *Gouverneur de Rouville* (Rouvilleweg 9, Otrabanda, Waterfront De Rouvilleweg, Willemstad) for good European cuisine.

Farther east is the Salina district and beaches where there is good food, as well as nightlife. Chinese shops known locally as 'snacks' are found around here, as well as in the town proper, while all top Curaçao hotels come with excellent restaurants. Many of the best accommodations with eateries reside around Mambo and Kontiki beaches.

Shopping and Leisure

Willemstad is known for its duty-free shopping in downtown Curaçao. The 57-acre Duty Free Zone at the harbor is said to be the biggest of its kind in the Caribbean. You can buy fine European goods including jewelry, watches, and fabrics, at the stores here, but you will need to have them delivered to your ship, plane, or indeed mailed directly home. Shops are usually closed on Sundays.

No sales tax and low duty keep prices down elsewhere in Curaçao, but the island is not especially known for its bargains. It is, however, pleasant to wander around the friendly souvenirs and crafts shops in Willemstad, and there are several markets. The main one is the Floating Market in Punda (eastern side), just around the corner from the multicolored houses. Although mainly visited for fresh produce, there are also some knick-knack stalls, plus it's an experience to see the boats. You can barter, but don't expect rock bottom prices.

Popular buys in Curaçao include: Dutch Delft china, jewelry, watches, linens, leather goods, Italian silks, French perfumes, Curaçao liqueur and Gouda cheese wheels. You can also pick up quintessential Dutch souvenirs, like clogs (the traditional Dutch wooden shoes), woodcarvings, and lacework.

Spas

Many of the hotels that preside over the beaches in Curaçao are spa resorts. Breezes Resort Spa & Casino is one of the most popular, positioned as it is on Kontiki Beach. Santai Spa at the Lions Dive & Beach Resort is also good and offers massages right on the beach, as well as luxurious treatments in-house. These spas are both in Willemstad, while farther south at the Barbara Beach Hyatt Regency Golf Resort is Atabei Spa, which takes its inspiration from the Arawak people.

Culture: sights to visit

Main attractions of Curacao are concentrated in the metropolitan area, but you can find many interesting excursion sites in and around Willemstad. Among historic sites of the capital beautiful colonial buildings has to be mentioned, as well as eight of castles that have managed to preserve perfectly to this day. The most beautiful ones are considered castles of Nassau and Amsterdam, until recently these powerful fortifications protected the island from pirates and invaders. Among iconic attractions of Willemstad there are three old bridges bearing names of Dutch queens.

The most famous cultural institution is considered Curacao Museum, which represents a priceless collection of art and antiquities. One of museum's halls is dedicated to the collection of old paintings, and in the other you can see the beautiful antique furniture. Among those represented in the museum, there are exhibits of antique maps, as well as items of Indian art.

An important object of the tour is the Senior winery that all guests of the island try to visit. It produces the Curacao liquor. Visitors of the winery will have an opportunity to observe the process of drink production. Winery is located in the beautiful 19th-century mansion. Traditionally the tour ends with liquor tasting

In the neighborhood of the capital there is the famous natural attraction – Hatok caves. Curious travelers are attracted to these places by the prospect of seeing huge stalactites and incredibly beautiful underground lake. Main inhabitants of the caves are colonies of bats; tour participants will be able to learn a lot of interesting facts about lives of these amazing creatures

Another famous natural landmark is located in the western part of Curacao. Beautiful Christoffel Park becomes a habitat for many animals and birds; during a walk around the reserve you can see iguanas and rabbits, white-tailed deer and lizards, as well as donkeys and exotic birds. A high tower was built in the reserve especially for tourists, so you can enjoy the natural splendor from a viewing platform. At the entrance to the reserve there is the Museum of Natural History that organizes amazing tours every day

Traditions & lifestyle

Curacao is home to more than a hundred of ethnic groups, so culture of the island is very versatile and diverse. Many national traditions remain unchanged for many centuries, the main aspect of life remain strong and trusting relationships between members of different communities. Indigenous people are very careful to nature and environmental issues are paramount to them. They haven't an abundance of resources on the island, but local residents appreciate and cherish every drop of the precious nature

Music and dance are vivid manifestations of national culture; they are feature a strong rhythmic foundation. In contrast to many other countries on the region, where the main musical instruments are drums and other percussion instruments, locals here are used to set the rhythm by their own hands. A few deft hand claps and the rhythm is set; local residents don't require any additional devices for fun and dancing

Strolling through local markets and souvenir shops, visitors can see a lot of interesting crafts, colorful fabrics and souvenirs. At first glance, they may resemble children's crafts, and there is a grain of truth in this association. The inherent 'childishness' of the local craft is due to the fact that original manufacturers were younger family members. While the parents were working on plantations, children were making colorful souvenirs to sell them later and to contribute to the well-being of the family

Multi-ethnic culture is also reflected in particularities of the language. It is a complex mix of Portuguese, Dutch, Spanish and Indian linguistic characteristics. The local dialect is very different from that which is inherent to residents of neighboring islands. Religious culture is also very versatile; adherents of different religions could be found on the island. Religious traditions differ with ritual elements, which are particularly demonstrated during various holidays.

Local people are very nice and friendly to foreigners, latest are treated with respect and some share of curiosity. Many natives may seem rather lazy and slow, when in fact they are hard-working and dutiful. Despite the inherent sociability and curiosity of locals, they are very considerate and polite. During intercourse you shouldn't worry about wrong question, as natives have excellent sense of delicacy, as well as a great sense of humor

Nightlife

Curacao is popular among fans of diving and beach holiday. It is a beautiful island with beautiful beaches and an abundance of entertainment options. The most suitable destination for snorkeling is Playa Kalki cove. The main attraction of this place is considered the underwater coral wall; during the dive divers can see lobsters, green eels, reef fish and other typical inhabitants of the underwater world. Not only divers, but also those who want to relax on a quiet and beautiful beach would enjoy the bay.

Not far from San Nicolas there is a place called 'Mushroom Forest.' This dive site is a network of caves and tunnels inhabited by exotic fish and turtles. The valley of Porto Marie is also an attractive dive site; those who wish to admire the rare marine life are sure to go there. In 1984, the Seaquarium was opened on the island, since than the complex has become a favorite tourist destination. There visitors can appreciate the diversity of inhabitants of the underwater world, feed turtles and rays, see the collection of the Museum and go diving - the choice of entertainment programs here is really amazing. Younger guests will be offered to get acquainted with inhabitants of the deep sea, take a picture with some animals and touch them.

Fans of outdoor recreation can spend their time in traditional activities: walking through beautiful natural places, jeep safaris, horseback riding and cycling. The most famous entertainment center is located in Willemstad. In Curacao Dolphin Academy visitors will be able to watch enchanting dolphin shows and swim with animals in the pool as well as try some interesting rides

Riffort Village mall is a great place for a family vacation. There are play areas for children of all ages there, as well as the cozy seating areas for their parents. Fans of golf have to visit the Old Quarry center. Here they have not only a high quality course, but also well-planned infrastructure. It has an equipment rent center, a sports shop and a stylish restaurant with a bar. The most colorful landmarks of nightlife are located in the capital. Clubs like Sopranos Plano and Zen are worth noting

Transportation
Curaçao Taxis and Car Rental

Taxis are metered and quite pricey though they can be shared from the airport and picked up at Curaçao hotels and the taxi rank at Punda. Fares go up after 8:00 p.m. and again at 11:00 p.m., and there are extra charges for luggage. Tips are expected (about 10 percent).

Taxis are denoted by a 'TX' on the license plate and will also oblige an island tour, charged by the hour. Note though, it is better to rent a car if you fancy seeing Curaçao. Visitors can use the central taxi service (+599-9-869-0752) or hail a cab from the Other Side (Otrobanda). For transfers and tours, try *Taber Tours* (+599-9-868-7012).

You won't need a taxi for getting around the downtown area, although Willemstad is quite spread out and the beaches are a fair way from the main sights. Car rental is available with Avis, Budget, Hertz, and some other companies, and you can pre-book online to pick up your vehicle at the airport. Most require drivers to be a minimum of 25 years old.

Curaçao Water Taxis

There are two cruise ship terminals in Willemstad, including the Mega Pier where tourists are deposited. The town proper is within easy reach of the Curaçao ports. Ferries provide transport around Schottegat harbor, and a short service runs across the channel when the Queen Emma Bridge is open for extended periods. This ferry goes between Punda and Otrobanda, is cheap, and takes just minutes.

Curaçao Buses

Public buses run around the island and city. There are two main services; the large Konvoi and the BUS (up to 12 passengers). Konvoi have standard fares to main landmarks in Willemstad and clear schedules, while the BUS runs more like a taxi in that you can negotiate where it goes. Be sure to ask the driver of the latter if they will be making a stop near your destination before getting on.

There are bus stations on the Otrobanda and Punda sides (on the west and east, respectively). To head to the Salina district, which is east of Curaçao, leave from Punda station. Otrobanda serves the western districts and the airport though there's no direct connection between the two.

Look for the 'Bushalte' bus stop signs or wave a bus down whenever you see one approaching. Services typically run between 6:00 a.m. and 8:00 p.m., or later in high-trafficked areas such as between downtown and Salina. Both services are cheap though neither is particularly efficient or comfortable.

Airports

Curaçao's airport, Hato International is located a few miles to the north of Willemstad and brings in passengers from North and South America, Europe, and the Caribbean. There are direct flights from the likes of Miami (American Airlines), as well as Newark, while direct services from Europe's Amsterdam with KLM and Arkefly, and from Dusseldorf with Air Berlin are also available. Hato International Airport handles more than a million passengers each year.

Shuttles arrive from nearby Aruba and Bonaire (the other members of the 'ABC'), as well as from the main countries in the Caribbean, including Jamaica (Montego Bay). It is not cheap to fly to Curaçao and all departing passengers have to pay a departure tax, apart from KLM fliers.

Hato International Airport has just one, recently built terminal which has good facilities. Arrivals, Departures, and Check-in are all easy to navigate and the airport has bridges to the planes. Inside are ATMs, a currency exchange, information desks (where English is spoken), and Wi-Fi. There is also decent shopping, including duty-free, where you can buy liquor, cigarettes, and perfume. There are bars, cafés, and restaurants if you get hungry.

Taxis to the downtown Curaçao and resorts run 24 hours from just outside arrivals or call +599-9-869-0752. They are quite expensive so you can share one if you are traveling by yourself or as a couple. Minivans also serve the airport, as do private shuttle buses provided by the top hotels so it pays to check if your hotel offers a transfer service. Cheap Autobus Busbedrijf Curaçao public buses also serve the facility.

For car rental, Budget, Avis, Alamo, National, Thrifty, and Hertz all have desks at Hato International Airport and vehicles can be pre-booked online. All budgets and types of vehicle can be found, with prices a bit higher than the US Eastern Seaboard cities. Willemstad is seven miles away, about a 15 minute drive to the south via Franklin D. Rooseveltweg, while Mambo Beach is slightly father and requires crossing over the Queen Juliana Bridge.

Visas and Vaccinations

Most visitors can enter Curaçao without a visa, including those from the US, Canada, the UK, the Netherlands and other European countries. Passports are typically stamped for stays of 30 days, on the condition that accommodation and flights are pre-booked. Unless you're coming from a high risk yellow fever region, vaccinations are not necessary.

Health and Safety

The sun, mosquitoes, and unhygienic food are the main health risks, although problems can be avoided with common sense. The people are generally friendly and helpful, and although crime is not endemic, car crime and drug-related theft can be problematic. Avoid driving at night and in out-of-the-way downtown areas.

It is hot year-round in Curaçao so always use sun block and wear good sunglasses when at the beach or sightseeing. Mosquitoes are an issue in the interior, with reports of dengue fever among the local populace. Try to cover up at night (avoid wearing black) and use mosquito repellant, particularly on the ankles.

Tap water, which is distilled sea water on Curaçao, is potable though most people stick with bottled water. Restaurants are hygienic for the most part, but visitors should only eat from street vendors where they can see the food being cooked and where it is served piping hot. There have been incidences of tourists contracting ciguatera poisoning through eating certain reef fish.

Main beaches have lifeguards and many are sheltered, while northern beaches are fewer, rougher, and more remote, and therefore should be avoided by swimmers. Always carry water when hiking in Christoffel National Park. Local drivers can be unpredictable and aggressive, and country roads tight, so be extra careful when behind the wheel.

Weather

Curaçao is warm and sunny most of the year, and is also drier than most other Caribbean destinations on account of its position in the south and near the South American continent. The average yearly temperature is a balmy 81°F (27°C), with an average monthly rainfall of less than two inches. The high season spans December to April, while the low season runs from May to November.

Much of the rain in Curaçao falls during the high season, occurring mostly between October and February. However, it tends to rain mostly at night and is often still sunny during the day. This is the busiest time, when many visitors from northern regions escape to Curaçao for a winter holiday in the sun.

The weather during the low season is actually drier and hotter, which may please some visitors. A major benefit of visiting during the low season is that hotels may reduce their rates between 25 and 50 percent, with May and September traditionally the cheapest months. Be aware, however, that some restaurants and shops close early during this time as there are fewer tourists.

The Caribbean is known for attracting hurricanes although Curaçao lies just outside the so-called hurricane belt so it typically does not bear the brunt of these storms. It can get hit by tropical storms, however, and there may also be offshoots from hurricanes in the region from June through November.

Best Time to Visit Curaçao

The weather is typically nice in Curaçao so there is no real best time to visit. High season here follows the same pattern as high season in the rest of the Caribbean, from the middle of December through the middle of April. This coincides with the end of the hurricane season and is a popular time with Americans seeking winter sun on Christmas or Spring break.

The diving is good year-round and trade winds make for good sailing. January through February is an ideal time to visit for the Curaçao Carnival, which is an extravaganza that draws big crowds.

Holidays and Festivals

Visitors can enjoy a variety of sporting events, music festivals, and the best of Caribbean culture throughout the year in Curaçao. Many events incorporate parades, with the most prominent being the annual Carnival, at the start of the year. The Curaçao North Sea Jazz Festival in late August is another must-see for music aficionados.

Curaçao Carnival (Carnaval)

Starting New Year's Day, Carnaval is the main Curaçao holiday event of the year and goes on through all of January. It features music, parades, and parties galore across all cultures that make up the island—Dutch, Portuguese, African, South American, and Jewish. There are also beauty contests and concerts, with the Festival di Tumba parade on Shrove Tuesday being the highlight.

Curaçao Heineken Regatta

Sponsored by a mega-brewer, the Curaçao Heineken Regatta is a fun, sporty high season event in late January. The international regatta sets off from Willemstad and goes over three days. While sailors race for a substantial dollar prize, on land are beach barbecues and parties.

International Kite Festival

Though not a must, the Curaçao International Kite Festival in February is worth a look as it highlights the creativity of the islanders. Along with flying and competitions which feature weird and wacky designs, are workshops where novices can learn to make and fly kites.

Curaçao Dive Festival

Curaçao is right up there with other areas of this region of the Caribbean for its scuba diving potential, and this festival in May has classes and dives for beginners and expert divers alike. Take note though, while this is the best time to dive in Curaçao, good visibility is apparent year-round.

Curaçao Restaurant Week

A great event for tourists in the low season, Restaurant Week sees hundreds of restaurants in Curaçao partake in the offering delicious three-course meals at a great value. The event spans over a week and is the perfect opportunity to taste Curaçao cuisine without breaking the bank.

Salsa Tour

The week-long Salsa Tour in August draws some of the best names in the business and features live concerts and workshops on the beach. Together with dance are scuba diving and snorkeling events, along with horseback rides.

Curaçao North Sea Jazz Festival

This two-day North Sea Jazz Festival in Piscadera Bay is the most high profile jazz festival in Curaçao. It features visiting artists from around the world who perform at the World Trade Center grounds, to the west of Willemstad. Along with jazz is a week of soul, hip hop, and R&B, leading up to the main event on August 31.

Amstel Curaçao Race

A mini Tour de France on Curaçao, the 50-mile long (80 km) Amstel Curaçao Race is run at the beginning of the high season in November, and usually attracts some big names in cycling. From Willemstad, the peloton goes around the island, with presentations at the Lions Dive & Beach Resort.

Saba
History & Culture

History & Culture Saba's birth was traumatic. Circa 500,000 BC the island was formed as the top of a volcano that became active during the middle of the late Pleistocene era. Now a dormant volcano, she has not erupted for about 5,000yrs.

Circa 1175 BC - hunter gatherers called Ciboney are considered to be the earliest settlers on Saba. They lived near Fort Bay where recent radiocarbon samples showed that the site is over 3,000yrs old.

Circa 800 AD - Arawak Indians migrated into the Caribbean basin from South America and built villages on Saba.

Fast forwarding to 1493, Christopher Columbus sighted the Unspoiled Queen, but sailed on by without attempting any sort of landing when he observed the treacherous nature of her jagged volcanic shores.

A century and a half later in 1632 the island welcomed her first European visitors, a group of shipwrecked Englishmen, they reported later that the island was inhabited. Recently found artifacts revealed the existence of Amerindian settlements.

In 1640, the Dutch West Indian Company, which had already settled on the neighboring island of St. Eustatius (known then as "The Golden Rock" as it was a thriving regional center of commerce) brought people over to Saba in order to colonize the island. Soon after, those Dutchmen were chased away by the famous British pirate Henry Morgan, due to the ongoing conflict between the Netherlands and Britain. For almost 200 years the island switched hands between The Dutch, Spanish, French and English. During this period the village of "The Bottom" was established 1200ft up from Fort Bay. Today it is the administrative center and capital of the island.

After much toing and froing the Dutch won out in 1816. For almost two centuries this still remains the case. Like everywhere else in the Caribbean, the tragedy of slavery brought people of African descent to Saba's shores, because life on the island was hard and all had to work together to survive, slavery on Saba ended far in advance of other parts of the world.

For many years Saba was known as a haven for Caribbean pirates. As time passed by the Unspoiled Queen wove her calming spell and the inhabitants, of Dutch, African, English, Scottish and Irish descent, many of the men became sailors and fishermen. These professions would see many of the Saba men away from the island for extended periods of time... The island thus became known as "The Island of Women"! Since the "man of the house" was often away Saba's women became very resilient and independent by necessity. Their renown grew for making socks, shoes, belts, gloves, Panama style straw hats and, still an enduring tradition today and a healthy income gained from export then, lace. Originally known as "Spanish work" the Sabans made it their own and "Saba Lace" is still created and can be purchased in several locations around the island today.

During this time the inhabitants spread to various locations on the island and formed the villages that we know today, where the fertile volcanic soil created ideal conditions for another profession... agriculture. From 1829 schools were established by the local churches to educate Saba's youth.

The Twentieth Century
Admiral E.A. JohnsonIn 1909 A navigational school was established by Frederick Simmons to train young Saban men in the ways of the sea.

Until 1943, transportation on Saba was not easy, steep trails between the sea and the settlements on the hills were negotiated on foot and donkey. Finally, in 1943, Josephus "Lambee" Hassell achieved the road that, Dutch & Swiss engineers claimed "couldn't be built". Hassell simply took a correspondence course in civil engineering and started to build the road with the help of his fellow islanders. Between 1943 & 1958 the road was completed in stages, the final stage being the road to Flat Point the future location of Saba's airport.

The first aircraft landing was in 1959 and an airport was opened in 1963 linking the island to St. Maarten. Finally, the construction of a pier in 1972 allowed not only fishing boats, but also sailboats and dive boats to moor, thus opening up the island to the possibility of tourism. It wasn't until the late 80's that Saba's Tourism industry started to grow.

The Saba Conservation Foundation (SCF) is a non-profit, non-governmental organization (NGO) and was established in 1987, with the main objective of preserving and managing Saba's Natural and cultural heritage. As previous generations of Saba people had appreciated the island's natural resources, the SCF was not conceived to repair damaged habitats, but rather to ensure the continued quality of an extraordinary environment for the benefit and enjoyment of all.

The Twenty First Century

Formally part of the Netherlands Antilles, Saba became part of a Special municipality of the Kingdom of the Netherlands together with the islands of St. Eustatius and Bonaire in 2010.

Today Saba's guests will discover a mixed population of European, African and Latin descendents, speaking English, Dutch and Spanish. Saban houses are well kept, the gardens team with flowers and the doors seldom are locked. The friendliness of Sabans is not in any doubt, and everyone knows everybody on the Unspoiled Queen

Travel and Tourism

Travel Guide

Renowned as the "unspoiled Queen" of the Caribbean, Saba is one of the more unique islands in Central America. The island is actually part of the Netherlands despite being many thousands of miles away from the European nation. It is found upon an active volcano called Mt Scenery. As a result, the landscape is lusciously green, with sparkling townships located around the mountain. Tourism is the center of the island's economy. Over the past decade, eco-tourism has become the forefront of Saba's global recognition.

Saba is famous for its unique landscape. Unlike other islands in the Caribbean, Saba has a coastline which is extremely rocky, instead of sandy. This led to its late colonization, as sailors refused to moor their ships close to the dangerous coast. Nevertheless, since colonization by the Dutch, Saba has continued to grow, but it wasn't until the 20th century that modern developments brought tourism to the island. Roads and ports made it possible for tourists to explore the natural richness of this tiny Caribbean jewel. Today, Mount Scenery is the heart of the island's tourism industry. However, diving is also popular, and so too is hiking. However, eco-tours are now the main focus of many travelers to Saba.

There is a small selection of resorts on the island and numerous cottages that can be rented out by the day or week. Most of the accommodation is found in the towns of Windwardside and The Bottom. For cheaper options, there are guesthouses which have shared common rooms, but are still very comfortable. The nightlife doesn't usually go on all night, with relaxation rather than pumping music the focus here. The food in Saba is tremendous. Seafood is fresh and delicious, but so too are the Western, European, and Asian cuisines found on the island. Whatever you eat, don't forget to wash it down with the local rum.

Saba is in the Caribbean Sea, and experiences a tropical maritime climate. Like other islands in the Leeward Antilles, Saba has hot summers and mild winters. During the year, an average temperature of 80°F blankets the island. The summer months are from June to August and are generally much hotter, more humid, and rainier than the winter months (December to February). Winter temperatures can fall to around 80°F, sometimes even lower. Rain falls more frequently between May and September, this period is prone to cyclones, which occur on a yearly basis around Saba and the Leeward Antilles.

The airport serving Saba is among the world's most fascinating. The runway is short, and only experienced pilots are recommended to fly here. Nevertheless, there are dozens of take-offs and landings every day. Flights connect to the larger Caribbean island of St Maarten, which is just a 15 minute flight away. American travelers cannot directly reach the island by air, but transfers are possible in both Antigua and St Maarten.

The island is small, but extremely beautiful. Therefore tourists are advised to take an hour or two to explore Saba upon 'The Road'. This is the only roadway on the island, which can be traveled by motorbike, car rental, taxi, or scooter.

Things to Do

Saba is a beautiful gem in the Caribbean Sea. Therefore it is naturally home to a stunning tropical landscape and reef system. Tourists can find a plethora of things to do on the island. Of course, Saba's surrounding reef system, which is protected by Saba National Marine Park, is the first thing tourists usually visit when they arrive. The reef is one of the most inspiring underwater environments in the Caribbean Sea, with scuba diving, unsurprisingly, one of Saba's premier tourist activities.

The island's beauty also extends away from the water. The green landscape, which is filled with rolling hills and clouded summits, is the perfect place for hiking. Tourists with a sense of adventure can find a number of trekking paths across Saba. Novices, experts, and every hiker in between will enjoy a few days' hiking on Saba.

Saba is home to an amazing reef system that surrounds the entire island. Diving has become a main contributor to the local tourism economy, and visitors will find dozens of reliable dive shops offering scuba diving equipment and reef tours. Saba is home to wall reefs and a host of other diving attractions, including Ladder Labyrinth, Third Encounter, and Man of War Shoals. Some of the dive sites are found just off-shore, although there are others that are further away. *Saba Divers* is as reliable as operators come.

If scuba diving doesn't interest tourists, but a need for visiting the underwater wonders of Saba is still lurking, then visitors can try snorkeling instead. Some areas of the Saba coastline are too dangerous for snorkeling, as rock walls and strong currents pose threats for even the strongest swimmers. This is why tourists should snorkel in safe beach areas and talk to local dive shops before doing so. *Sea Saba* offers snorkeling tours of the island.

Eco-tourism is an important part of the island. The beautiful landscape makes it possible to go hiking. Mount Scenery is the first place tourists should hike to. However, there are some 18 different trekking spots across the island, including several challenging treks as well as easy paths. There are a number of travel agencies offering hiking tours of Saba and its luscious landscape, including *Viator*.

Even though the water and landscape make for the most popular tours of Saba, tourists should not overlook town tours. There are four villages on the island that radiate intriguing atmospheres. Windwardside and The Bottom are the two largest towns, offering a host of colonial buildings that are ideal for sightseeing. Even the smaller villages of Hell's Gate and St. John's are great for exploring as they are tiny communities with a range of interesting architecture. *Get Your Guide* has great deals on sightseeing in the towns.

It is possible to find boating tours on the island. Even though the island of St Maarten is where most of the region's boat charters originate, the local fishing boats and diving tours of Saba can take your around the island. *Definitive Caribbean* is a travel group that provides access to boat charters and dive boats in Saba.

Attractions

Saba may not be the largest island in the Caribbean, but it is bursting with many amazing attractions. The island is home to a rich diversity of fauna and flora which adds to the scenic landmarks like Mount Scenery, the highest summit in the Lesser Antilles. Of course, there are also the underwater marvels of Saba that lure tourists from across the region. Saba National Marine Park is 'swimming' with a seemingly endless variety of tropical aquatic species.

Mount Scenery

Commonly regarded as the most important landmark on the island, Saba's Mount Scenery is the 2,700-foot mountain located just outside Windwardside. The mountain is the tallest landmark in the former Netherlands Antilles and one of the most visited natural destinations in the Caribbean. Hiking up the mountain means tourists will have to climb the 1,000 steps that have been chiseled out of the cliff. No matter what time of the year, hikers summiting the mountain will need some cool-weather gear. The weather at the peak is foggier and chillier than at sea-level, but some magnificent wildlife awaits visitors. Address: Mount Scenery, Windwardside, Saba, Caribbean

Well's Beach
Saba does not contain beautiful sandy beaches as the island is surrounded by rocky outcrops and sheer cliff faces. However, there are plenty of swimming opportunities around the island. One of the best spots along the coastline is Well's Beach. It is home to a small, black-sanded beach that provides an opportunity for sun-baking. However, swimming is the more popular past-time here for locals and tourists alike. Of course, snorkeling just off the beach area is a safe and intriguing activity for people visiting the area. Address: Well's Bay, Saba, Caribbean Netherlands Phone: n/a Website: n/a

Harry L. Johnson Memorial Museum
One of the more interesting, yet often overlooked, landmarks on the island is the Harry L. Johnson Memorial Museum, which is found in Windwarside. The museum is found inside one of the old colonial houses of Windwardside, which only adds to the majestic spectacle of the site. The house once belonged to a sea captain, but now contains a range of historical artifacts about Saba. These items include Native

Indian relics, colonial records, and historical decor. The museum is open from 10:00 a.m. to 4:00 p.m. but there is a two-hour lunch break at midday. Address: Windwardside, Saba, Caribbean Netherlands

Website:http://www.sabatourism.com/museums.html

Saba Marine Park
Saba Marine Park encompasses the area of water around the island, where tourists can explore the many reefs and rocky outcrops by snorkeling, diving, or simply boating. Visitors are permitted to enter the marine park without charge, unlike other places around the world's tropical region. The oceanic marine environment that surrounds Saba is outstanding. There is a huge range of sea creatures residing just off the coast of Saba, including tropical fish, crustaceans, and sharks. **Address:** Saba Marine Park, Saba

Flat Point Tide Pools
The Tidal Pools at Flat Point is more than just an interesting spot at the end of a hiking trail. It consists of numerous rock pools of different sizes, wedged between the ocean and a cliff face. Tourists can spend hours exploring the different size tidal pools, which are all home to a wondrous array of sea creatures. It is recommended that visitors check with local guides before reaching the tidal pools as they are only seen at certain times of the day and at certain times of the year. Address: Flat Point, Saba

Hilltop Spa Retreat

Many of Saba's attractions require a lot of energy from tourists to enjoy. Therefore it is nice to find a place to relax and unwind. On Saba, the Hilltop Spa Retreat is one of the best features of the island. Offering beautiful views over the island, plus excellent spa services, this venue is where tourists can meditate, practice yoga, or relax with a massage. Prices are reasonable, but budget travelers may want to skip this landmark. Address: Hilltop Spa Retreat, Saba, Caribbean Netherlands

Tent Reef Wall

There are plenty of fascinating dive sites located around the island. However, one that commonly stands out among the others is Tent Reef Wall. What makes this site popular is its landscape, which was formed by a heavy lava flow down a sea ledge. At the wall, divers are able to come face to face with unique sea creatures, including sea turtles, urchins, and sponges. The best way to get here is by visiting one of the dive centers around the island and then traveling with a dive group. Address: Tent Reef Wall, Saba

Saba Artisan Foundation

Found in the town of The Bottom, the Saba Artisan Foundation is where tourists can explore the beautiful artwork of the island. Lacework is one of the more popular displays inside this center.

However, there is also a beautiful array of ceramics and paintings to be viewed or even purchased. The Artisan Foundation is open daily between 8:00 a.m. and 5:00 p.m. although there is a two-hour lunch break starting at midday. Address: Saba Artisan Foundation, The Bottom, Saba, Caribbean Netherlands

Food and Restaurants

The restaurants on the island of Saba are high in number and generally offer fine dining experiences for patrons. Of course, most of the restaurants are found in Windwardside and The Bottom. However, there are also plenty of hotels and resorts around the island which boast tremendous restaurants and bars for tourists to enjoy. Even though the island is small, there are European, Caribbean, American, and Asian influences in Saba's wide range of restaurants. There are some traditional dishes that shouldn't be overlooked, including calaloo soup, breadfruit, and curried goat. Bars and lounges are available, but generally close around midnight, or not long after. Saba Spice is the local rum. It can be quite potent, so drinkers need to be careful when sampling it.

Bars and Pubbing in Saba

Windwardside is the place to be when looking for a night venue. However, Saba's nightlife is generally quiet. *Scout's Place Bar* (Scout's Place Hotel, Windwardside) has some of the best views on the island and provides a splendid atmosphere for locals and tourists alike. Although a renowned restaurant, *Tropics Café* (Windwardside) is also a great spot for happy hour beers every evening except Monday. *Saba's Treasure* (Windwardside) is more than just a restaurant as it has a fully-equipped sports bar on site.

Outside of Windwardside, there are several spots to enjoy a drink or two. In the town of St John's, the *Midway Bar and Restaurant* (St John's) has great food and a social atmosphere. The aptly named *Half Way Bar* (St John's) is found between the two largest towns of Saba. It is small yet tourists can enjoy the social life here. Like the name suggests, *Sunset Bar* (Ladder Bay) is the ideal pub to sit back after a long day of sightseeing and enjoy the receding sunlight.

Dining and Cuisine in Saba

Windwardside is where many of the island's restaurants are located. *Brigadoon* (Windwardside) is the best restaurant on Saba, offering lobster, steak, chicken, seafood, and pork dishes to die for. French cuisine is enticing, but none more so than at *Eden* (Lambee's Place, Windwardside). This is also a perfect place to spend a romantic dinner for two. *Saba's Treasure* (Windwardside) is a mixture of excellent dining and historical treasures. The owner of *Brigadoon* (Windwardside), Greg Johnson, is currently creating an improved dining environment at *Saba's Treasure* (Windwardside).

The *Saba Coffee House* (The Bottom) is the spot for a refreshing coffee, an ideal lunch, or a bistro dinner experience. *Queen's Serving Spoon* (The Bottom) offers traditional food made from the freshest ingredients. Another popular establishment for all-day dining is *Lollipop* (The Bottom), which is a small venue that boasts a wonderful menu.

Outside the towns of The Bottom and Windwardside, Saba contains several important dining options. *In Two Deep* (Fort Bay) is a nice little restaurant located close to Fort Harbor Bay. In the town of Hell's Gate, *The Gate House* (Hell's Gate) is another interesting restaurant away from the crowds of The Bottom and Windwardside.

Shopping and Leisure

Tourists will not find major shopping malls or even historic markets on the island of Saba. Instead, tourists are greeted with local products. Shopping is not the same as one would find in the United States or other Westernized countries. Stores generally open between 8:00 a.m.

and midday, then again from 2:00 p.m. to 6:00 p.m. Monday to Saturday. There are several products that are worth checking out while holidaying on Saba. Embroidery is an important traditional handicraft. In addition, local art and crafts are popular items to take home.

Embroidery
The most popular and perhaps most historically important piece of merchandise for the local economy is Saban lace. There are several spots on the island that boasts incredible Saban lace products, not to mention a range of other fabric-related goods like garments. Island Craft Shop in the town of Windwardside, the stunning little Saban Lace Boutique in Hell's Gate, and the Saba Artists' Foundation in The Bottom are the main places where these products can be found.

Arts and Crafts
Local art, not just from Saba but from a variety of islands around the Caribbean, is another major lure for visitors. The best venue to find art is at Windwardside's Peanut Gallery. In addition to paintings, tourists will find ceramics and other fabulous pieces of work for sale here.

Property
Recent years have seen an increase in foreign property investment on the island. There is a huge range of houses and lodgings for sale in Saba, including houses, cottages, and expensive villas. Whether

tourists would like to become permanent residents or are looking for a tropical property for investment purposes, Saba has a range of choices available.

Transportation
Saba Taxis and Car Rental
There is only one road that meanders through the island. It is called 'The Road' for obvious reasons and passes through the four conurbations of Saba. Taxis are regarded as the best way to get from one town to another, and are recommended instead of walking as the road can be dangerous and hilly. Tourists won't feel like they are being ripped off when using taxi services as rates are closely regulated. Many taxi services operate in Saba, including *Taxi Billy* (+559-416-6260) and *Taxi Eddy Peterson* (+559-416-2640).

Rental cars are another great option for getting around quickly on Saba. However, it is more expensive to rent a car than it is to use the extensive taxi services on the island. However, car rental is recommended for tourists who want to travel a lot during their island stay. Several car rental services are available, including *Kenny's Rental*, *Caja's Car Rental*, and *Johnson's Rent-A-Car*.

Saba Water Taxis

Getting to the island is possible via boat from St Maarten. There are two vessels that make the journey to Saba: *The Edge* and *Dawn II*. On Tuesdays, Thursdays, and Saturdays, *Dawn II* travels to Saba from St Maarten. However, *The Edge* departs St Maarten for Saba each day between Wednesday and Sunday.

Saba Trains and Buses

There are no train services on this small island and buses are also non-existent due to the fact that the single road is too small to safely accommodate buses. Nevertheless, there are plenty of ways to get around Saba, including motorbikes, scooters, hitchhiking, car rental, and taxis.

Airports
Juancho E. Yrausquin Airport
There is only one airport operating on the island of Saba. It has international facilities, but flights only come in from the nearby islands of St Maarten and Saint Eustatius. However, this doesn't stop the airport from boasting a global reputation. This is because the runway is one of the world's most dangerous landing and take-off strips. Winair is the only air carrier operating from Juancho E. Yrausquin Airport. Flights generally take about 12 to 15 minutes to reach St Maarten, from where connecting flights to the US mainland can be

found. Apart from the helicopter journeys to and from the island, connections are made via prop-aircraft rather than jet-engine carriers. This is because the runway is dangerously short, measuring at less than 400 meters.

The terminal building is only basic and small. It was built in 1963 and contains a limited number of facilities. Tourists can use a public phone booth and there is one information counter, which is also used as a check-in desk. There are no shopping and food services in the terminal, but several offices for Winair.

Getting from the airport to the villages of Saba is best done by taxi. Car rental is available on the island, but there are no car rental services directly at the airport. There is parking available at Juancho E. Yrausquin Airport.

Travel Tips

Language: Both English and Dutch are the two main languages spoken on the island. However, Dutch is the official language. Schools use both languages to teach the local curriculum.

Currency: US dollars is the currency used throughout Saba. It is advised that tourists bring US dollars to the island with them rather than another currency or travelers' checks, as the exchange rate is poor in Saba. MasterCard and Visa are widely accepted by hotels, some restaurants, and airlines. ATMs are not ubiquitous as they are only found in Windwardside and The Bottom. Banking hours on the island begin at 8:30 a.m. and end at 3:30 p.m. Monday to Friday. However, there are only three banks operating on Saba.

Time: Saba falls within the Atlantic Standard Time zone, which is four hours behind Coordinated Universal Time (UTC -4).

Electricity: Saba electricity comes at 220-240 Volts, which means North American travelers will need to bring a converter if they want to use American appliances here. European-style plugs are used in Saba, which are designed with two round pins. Therefore an adapter is also required by US travelers wishing to use appliances from home here.

Communications: +599 is the international dialing code for the islands of the Netherlands Antilles. However, to reach Saba, this code needs to be followed by 4 and then the local number. Phone networks on the island are operated by several companies, including Windward Cellular Network and East Caribbean Cellular. Phone booths can be found in the four main communities, and most resorts and hotels provide international long-distance calling services. The local post office is located at The Bottom, and Windwardside is the only destination that has an internet café. Most large hotels have internet connection.

Duty-free: Passengers must be 15 years or over to carry duty-free items into Saba. However, there are some restrictions. For tobacco products, passengers can bring in 200 cigarettes or 50 cigars. Alternatively, 250 grams of tobacco may be brought into Saba. When it comes to alcoholic beverages, two liters may be imported without paying duty.

Tourist Office: Saba Tourism Bureau, Windwardside: http://www.sabatourism.com/ or +599-4-16-2231

Emergency: Emergency services: +599-416-3237

Visas and Vaccinations

Travelers from North America do not need a visa to enter Saba for stays of less than three months. Initially most visitors are granted a 14-day stay, which can be extended to a three-month stay at Immigration. Visit http://travel.state.gov/visa/ to find out more about travel requirements to Saba. There are few health risks here but the usual precautions apply to those who plan to partake in adventurous activities such as diving or hiking.

Health and Safety

Saba's main cities are generally safe, but drug-related crime does exist therefore tourists should exercise caution when traveling at night and always use common sense.

The high humidity during the summer months means tourists are susceptible to heat exhaustion and other heat-related illnesses if they don't take care of themselves. Drinking plenty of water is advised and wearing loose yet protective clothing is recommended. While sightseeing and exploring the island, visitors should wear a hat to keep the sun's harmful rays off their head.

Tuberculosis and hepatitis B vaccinations are recommended, but not essential, before traveling to Saba. In the summer months, insect bites are a common problem as heavy rainfall helps increase insect populations on the island. Carry insect repellant at all times and ask your hotel for a mosquito net.

Weather

Saba is found in the Caribbean Sea, so it experiences a tropical maritime climate. Like other islands in the Leeward Antilles, Saba experiences hot summers and mild winters. During the year, an average temperature of 80°F blankets the island. Nevertheless, tourists will feel a difference between summer and winter on Saba.

The summer months (June through August) are generally much hotter, more humid, and rainier than the winter months (December to February). Temperatures exceed 88°F on average, and coupled with the humidity, don't make summer an overly comfortable holiday experience. Winter temperatures can fall to around 80°F, sometimes even lower. The mercury is more comfortable for holidaying during the cooler months.

Rain falls more frequently between May and September. In addition, this period is prone to cyclones, which occur on a yearly basis around Saba and the Leeward Antilles. The highland areas of the island experience cold temperatures, especially at night. This means tourists should carry warm clothes if spending the night atop places like Mt Scenery.

Best Time to Visit Saba
Saba is best visited during the winter months. However, this is also when the peak tourism season occurs. Many tourists from Europe and North America flock to the island during their bitterly cold winters at home in search of warm weather. December and January are particularly busy months in Saba, not to mention more expensive.

The summer months are humid and hot, bringing heavy rain, tropical storms, and cyclones. In addition, insects populate the island during the rainy period and can make sleeping uncomfortable for tourists. Nevertheless, April and October experience less humidity and fewer insect issues than summer, making tourism suitable at this time.

Holidays and Festivals

Saba's most popular festival is undoubtedly the Summer Festival, which is otherwise known as Carnival. The entire island becomes a swarming parade of color, dance, and excitement at this time. Like other parts of the Caribbean during Carnival, Saba becomes extremely crowded during this event. Another popular Saba holiday is Saba Days, which sees sporting competitions, dance performances, and barbecue feasts.

Easter
Easter is celebrated in March, and due to the high number of people that flock here during this time, reservations are recommended. Tourists should head to the local church on Saba, where celebrations are held for several days.

Coronation Day
On April 30, Saba celebrates the coronation and birthday of the Dutch royal Queen Beatrix. The day is a national holiday, so visitors should expect local banks and government offices to be closed. There is

always a welcoming celebration in The Bottom and Windwardside as Sabans hold the Dutch royal family in high regard.

Carnival

The most visited and liveliest festival on the island is Carnival. This event is also referred to as the Summer Festival and lures the largest crowds of any event every year. Book hotels in advance as accommodations tend to be overflowing when Carnival comes to the island. Parades, costumes, music, and the rhythms of steel drums dominate the processions through the streets of Saba. The event is held across the last week in July.

Sea and Learn Festival

The ocean and its marine environment are important for the local Saban community. To help teach visitors and locals alike about the significance of ocean conservation, the Sea and Learn Festival is held in October. Every year, scientists, naturalists, and professors from around the world flock to Saba to make presentations, hold exhibitions, and host shows about life in the surrounding waters. It is a great time for any tourists to visit Saba.

Saba Days

In December, Saba Days is held to showcase the beauty of this fantastic island. The festival is held in honor of the island and incorporates interesting cultural activities, including dancing, sports, and weekend-long barbecues. The fun and games are held across the island, in all of the villages. Nevertheless, The Bottom and Windwardside are usually the busiest spots on Saba during this event.

Christmas
Saba is a predominantly Roman Catholic island, so it is only natural that Christmas is celebrated here each year. The Sabans believe Christmas to be a big deal and performances are regularly held on the island leading up to the big day (December 25).

New Year's Eve
Tourists will be surprised by the beauty of Saba on New Year's Eve. There are plenty of spots for the crowds, so tourists have a lot of options for a New Year's Eve party on Saba. Of course, due to the many tourists who visit at this time, it is important to book hotels well in advance.

Travel information

All travel to Saba connects in St. Maarten.

Several major airlines from North America, Europe and South America carry daily flights into St. Maarten's Princess Juliana International Airport (SXM). Special charter flights are also available from major cities during the winter season. There are currently two airlines and two ferry services that operate schedules to Saba's shores from her international hub.

Departure Tax: An Airport and Harbor departure tax fee of $10.00 is payable when departing Saba. There are no ATM's at the airport and harbor.

By Air from St. Maarten:

Winair

(Windward Islands Airways) makes four or more flights each day to Saba to Juancho E. Yrausquin Airport. Inter-island flights can be arranged, some are scheduled weekly.

Book On-line: Passengers and travel agents can now make their Winair booking for any destination online and will receive an e-ticket for their travel. Go to www.fly-winair.com for online reservations and ticketing.

Johnson's Travel Services (On-Island Winair Agent)
Located on Saba, Johnson's Travel Services can answer your questions about prices, schedules and provide other helpful information about traveling to Saba with WINAIR. Whether planning a vacation or just a day trip to Saba contact:

Johnson's Travel Services

Juancho E. Yrausquin Airport

Flat Point

Saba

Dutch Caribbean

Tel: +599 416-2255

Email: winairsab@gmail.com.

Windward Express Airways (Private Air Charters)
Established in 2000 Windward Express Airways has become a leader in the private charter travel industry. Flying to client's schedule and destinations on time while avoiding air terminal check-in, line-ups and lost huggage. From a short flight to a personal itinerary, Windward Express Airways provides direct full access to international, regional and restricted airports (Saba, St. Barths, Baillif, Le Saints). Check with Windward Express Airways first.
Web: windwardexpress.com

By Sea from St. Maarten

Dawn II
Dawn II is based at Fort Bay, Saba, traveling three times a week to Dock Maarten Marina, Great Bay, Philipsburg, Sint Maarten.

Tuesdays, Thursdays, & Saturdays

Departs Saba at 7:00 am ~ Arrives Dock Maarten at 8:30 am

Departs Dock Maarten at 4:30 pm ~ Arrives Saba at 6:00 pm

Reservations Recommended. Check-in at least 30 mins. prior to departure to clear immigration.

The Dawn II features a fully air conditioned passenger cabin with comfortably padded seats inside, seating outside to enjoy the cool caribbean breeze andlots of space for luggage and dive gear!

Dawn II is available for private charters for private groups or island hopping.

Please contact Saba C-Transport, N.V. to make reservations or for additional information:

DAWN II ~ The Saba Ferry

Saba C-Transport, N.V.

Windwardside

Saba, Dutch Caribbean

Tel: +599-416-2299 Reservations

Tel:+599-416-6051 Emergency contact

Direct from the USA: (607) 8-GO-SABA

Web: **sabactransport.com**

Email: **info@sabactransport.com**

Find Us on Facebook: **sabactransport**

Follow us on Twitter: **sabactransport**

Skype Name: sabactransport

Agents for & DAWN II ~ The Saba Ferry & Mutty's Pride cargo vessel contact us for all your shipping needs!

The Edge (Wednesday, Friday, Sunday)

Travels to Saba from Sint Maarten (from Simpson Bay/Pelican Marina) on Wednesday, Friday and Sunday, departing Sint Maarten at 9:00 a.m. for the 1 hour 20 minute trip and returns from Saba, departing Fort Bay harbor at 3:30 p.m., arriving back on Sint Maarten at 5:00 p.m.

This means of transportation is good for travelers who overnight on Sint Maarten as well as a great way for any tourist to enjoy our wonderful nature island: incredible variety of hiking trails and renowned marine park. So whether you choose to hike, dive of just tour the island, The Edge is your ticket to get to this special island..

Prices: Daytrip is $100 per person including port fees. One way $65 per person. Children are half price. Check in is at 8:15 a.m. on SXM and departs sharp at 9 a.m. The trip from Saba to St. Maarten requires check in at 3 p.m.

Charters are also available for private groups. Capacity is 62 passengers.

Email: info@stmaarten-activities.com or info@seasaba.com - ask about their discounted inclusive price for ferry, diving, lunch and more
Website: www.stmaarten-activities.com

Please note prices and schedules do change, check with the operator before your trip.

Getting Around on Saba

Transportation on and around the island is made easy by our taxi drivers. Sit back and enjoy the ride and let your driver be your guide.

Saba Road

It's fair to say that not many places in the world can boast a road as an attraction. The Saba people challenge you to take a a 30-minute drive on 'The Road' to understand why Saba lives up to its nickname: "The Unspoiled Queen".

Buckle up when you depart Saba's renowned airport and enter Zion's Hill (A.k.a. Hell's Gate). As you wind and twist the chiseled cliff sides you may struggle to focus on the amazing panoramas of the neighboring islands, old fashion villages and varied seascapes. As you carve your way across the island, down the S-curve (pictured above and below), you find Saba's point of commerce, its only harbor the pulsing, Fort Bay. First gear to get back up to The Bottom (at 1,200 feet) in order to get down to you next stop, the illusive disappearing, reoccurring beach at Well's Bay.

Before the Road life on Saba was much tougher, Sabans faced the arduous task of traversing the island by trail, everything including the kitchen sink, pianos and monarchs were transported by hand and donkey through grueling elevations beneath the unforgiving Caribbean sun on twisting trails... So In the late 1930's the decision to build a concrete road was made. Dutch & Swiss Civil Engineers deemed it a foolhardy task due to the island's extreme topography. Thus the road got its title: "The road that couldn't be built."

Building "The road that couldn't be built".
Josephus Lambert Hassell (A.k.a. Lambee)Luckily for the island it was left to a Saban to make the much needed piece of infrastructure a reality... Josephus Lambert Hassell (A.k.a. Lambee) was clearly a man who had issues with the word "couldn't". Challenged by the word he followed a study in civil engineering by way of correspondence courses obtained by mail. In 1938, with the assistance of his fellow Sabans and no heavy machinery (yes it was all built by hand!) they got

down to the business of the impossible. The vital access road from Fort Bay to The Bottom was completed within 5 years! This first stage of the road was inaugurated in 1943. Four years later the first motor vehicle arrived

In 1951, the road to Windwardside and St. John's was opened and seven years later the road was completed. For two decades the islanders toiled to complete the project. Exercise caution before using the word "never" or the phrase "it can't be done" within earshot of a Saban.

Driving "The Road" is an experience in itself... A plethora of ecological zones await. Meandering from dry tundra up to dense tropical vegetation, winding past many steep drop offs as you go... The views are spectacular! Ascending the "Mountain Road", which ends at the Mt. Scenery trail, brings you to the highest point of the road which is over 1800ft above sea level! So don't be surprised whilst driving (or being driven) on Saba, to slip from bright warm sunshine into cool mystical cloud.

Hiking the road can be strenuous but rewarding, just remember to keep to the outside of the curves and away from inner rock faces and walls when rounding corners - to give traffic plenty of time to see you coming! If you run out of steam, take a seat on the wall and stick your thumb out, before too long someone will stop and offer you a ride.

Saba Port

Access to Saba from the sea is on the south east shore of the island at Saba's only port Fort Bay Harbor. The port was made more user friendly back in 1972 with the completion of the Captain Leo Chance Pier. Thus allowing larger vessels that the existing small pier couldn't facilitate to dock. Since then the Fort Bay has expanded and the facilities have improved dramatically.

The Port is the busiest place on the island as it is used by Local Fishermen, Dive Operators, Ferry Services and Shipping companies alike. Practically all of Saba's goods move through here so delivery day can be quite hectic! You're always guaranteed to hear the islands most colorful language on a busy day... You'll find the Harbor Office, Customs, Saba Marine Park, Gas Station (the only one on the island!), Three Dive shops, Two restaurants and the Island's Electricity generators at the Fort, generators that not only power the entire island, but add a soundtrack to the melee that heightens its energy (and acts as censor for some of that aforementioned "colorful language").

Ferry Services

Sailing to Saba is an opportunity not to be missed. As she looms ever closer upon the horizon you'll be distracted from her silhouette by nature, keen eyes will be rewarded by the sight of brown booby birds chasing flying fish, sprightly dolphins and the luckiest of voyager may even spy a breaching whale...

Two regular Ferry Services use the Port; the Dawn II Ferry which is based on Saba and The Edge Ferry run by Aquamania which is based on St. Maarten. Check in times from St. Maarten are 4.00 p.m. from Dock Maarten Marina, Great Bay, Philipsburg, for the Dawn & 8.00 a.m. at Pelican Marina for the Edge. The services do not run daily and are subject to change/weather conditions (as all travel is to Saba). Check out their web sites in our related links to get accurate up to date schedule information.

Information for Vessels visiting Saba*
Whilst coming ashore we strongly advise that you enter the island of Saba only through Fort Bay Harbor as the other areas (Well's Bay, Ladder Bay and Cove Bay) can be treacherous in certain sea conditions that may be deceptive from aboard your vessel.

Check-in procedures
Arriving yachts are required to proceed to the Fort Bay Harbor as soon as possible, clear Customs and Immigration, then check in/out with

the harbormaster to fulfill the required formalities. If Customs and Immigration are not available, proceed directly to the Harbor Office. The opening hours of the harbor office are from 6 AM to 6 PM. For your convenience and to speed up the procedures, the Customs and Immigration form can be downloaded in PDF format here.

Every yacht is ALSO REQUIRED to check in with the Marine Park at the office also located in Fort Bay. Download the yacht registration form (editable PDF format), or visit our downloads section.

Contact the Saba National Marine Park office (+599 416 3295) or Harbor Master on VHF channel 16 for directions on anchoring, mooring use, or any other information you may require.

St. Eustatius

St. Eustatius History

Eustatius, Sint Eustatius, also known as Statia or Statius, is a Dutch Caribbean island with a rich history. Statia or "Stay-sha"lies in the northern Leeward Islands portion of the West Indies, southeast of the Virgin Islands, immediately to the northwest of Saint Kitts & Nevis and to the southeast of Saba. The first inhabitants of Statia were the Saladoids, who arrived in sea faring canoes from South America before the end of the 15th century. The name of the island, "Sint Eustatius", is the Dutch name for Saint Eustace a legendary Christian martyr. The island was seen by Christopher Columbus in 1493 and claimed by many different nations. From the first settlement, in the 17th century until the early 19th century, St. Eustatius changed hands twenty-two times. In 1636, the Dutch West India Company took possession of St. Eustatius, Sint Maarten, and Saba which all fell under Dutch control. A commander was stationed on St. Eustatius to govern all three islands by 1678. Tobacco and sugar were also cultivated on the island during this period.

In the 1600's, slaves of African descent were brought to the island to cultivate the land, which had more than seventy plantations. During the 1700s, the capital, Oranjestad, was a major port for slave traders and merchants who came to trade slaves, sugar, and cotton. During the latter part of the 17th century and throughout the 18th century, St. Eustatius was a major trading center. In the 18th century, St. Eustatius' location in the middle of Danish, French, and Spanish territories served as a free port with no customs duties and its economy flourished. At this time, most all of the seafaring people knew of the "Golden Rock" as they called the island. By the end of the 18th century, slavery became outlawed in the Dutch Antilles. Formerly part of the Netherlands Antilles, Sint Eustatius became a special municipality within The Netherlands on 10 October 2010.

Geographically, St. Eustatius is mostly undeveloped volcanic island. Only 11 square miles with 2 volcanoes, 21 forts and outposts, a botanical garden, more than a dozen hiking trails in the Quill/Boven National Park, old cemeteries, a restored old town, and a marine park containing some of the best diving in the Caribbean. Much of its coastline is quite rugged but with some inns and restaurants for tourists to visit. Scuba divers are drawn to Statia to explore a hundred sunken ships, while others come to climb the Quill volcano and see the lush forest growing from its crater. In Oranjestad, you can visit historic Fort Oranje, the Dutch Reformed Church, and the St. Eustatius Historical Foundation Museum.

St. Eustatius helps to protect nature and the marine life. The St. Eustatius National Parks Foundation, known locally as Stenapa is responsible for helping to promote ecotourism and the appreciation of visiting such a beautifully natural island. Stenapa oversees the National Parks including The Quill is a dormant volcano with a tropical rainforest and the Boven Subsector which is an extinct volcano on the north end of the island. Stenapa is an environmental organization dedicated to preserving the marine/land environment and monitor and protect endangered species. One of Stenapa's marine projects was to create the St. Eustatius Marine Park that opened in 1998. The formation of the Marine Park helps preserve the underwater nature. The seas around Statia are considered amongst the most pristine in the world. The Marine Park covers the sea floor and the waters from the high water mark down to the 30-meter (100 ft.) depth. It encompasses areas from the Gallows Bay to White Wall area; from Jenkins Bay to North Point as well as Oranjebaai. To protect the coral reefs from damage, anchoring is not allowed in the Marine Park areas.

Today, people of more than 20 nationalities live in peace and harmony on this beautiful Dutch Caribbean Island. Many tourists visit the island each year as well to enjoy the beauty and splendor all around.

Tourism

Travel Guide

St Eustatius, a small yet significant country, has had a couple nicknames in the past, including the "historic gem" and the "golden rock," although today most people refer to the Caribbean island as simply "Statia," an abbreviation of its full name. It is a tropical island like no other, a true jewel steeped in history and culture. The island has not succumbed to over development like many other tropical beach destinations, making it an unrivaled nature retreat, with wonders to behold both on land and under the surrounding Caribbean Sea.

Diving is extremely popular here, and since the entire surrounds of the island is protected by a marine park, a little trip under the warm waters of the Caribbean can be a very rewarding experience. Visitors and locals alike also take to the waters by boat at every given opportunity, as the tranquil atmosphere of the Caribbean lends itself well to blissful and relaxing pastimes. Also not to be missed is a visit to the country's interior and hiking on the fertile slopes of the dormant volcano, an area abundant with wildlife.

The island is packed with comfortable, high standard accommodation as a result of its legacy as part of Europe. St Eustatius was colonized by the Dutch in the 17th century, and today remains part of the nation and shares its high standard of hospitality. The island has not been overrun with development like so many other Caribbean islands, and much of the accommodation here comes in the form of ex-colonial buildings with beautiful exteriors, while the interiors are modernized to today's standards. The locals, numbering just 3,500 people, are extremely friendly here, always greeting visitors with a warm Caribbean smile.

St Eustatius is a humid tropical island, with temperatures averaging about 80°F throughout the year. Seasonal variation is minor and temperatures never exceed 85°F. The rainy season in Martinique is August through December. April and June also experience mild showers, but these are generally short-lived. The best time to visit Srt. Eustatius is during the dry season, between December and April.

There are several enchanting dive spots located off St Eustatius in the Caribbean Sea, while boating and fishing are perhaps just as popular. The country has two wonderful National Parks: a dormant volcano known as the 'Quill', and a botanical garden on the slopes of the mountain. Both are a nature-lover's dream, and offer excellent hiking and birding opportunities. There are also several archeological dig sites around the island where you can discover more about the area's intriguing history.

The island has one airport, located in the capital city of Oranjestad. It is also possible to reach St Eustatius from the nearby island of St Maarten on a scheduled ferry service. The island itself is only eight square miles across, taking just an hour to circumnavigate by car. There are several car rental companies to choose from or, alternately, you can get around the island by taxi, which offer set, but reasonable, prices

Things to Do

Since St Eustatius is a tropical island in the Caribbean Sea, it is no surprise that the enticing warm waters provide excellent opportunities for water sports, such as diving, boating, and fishing. In fact, the entire island is surrounded by a marine park, which stretches from water level to 100ft below the surface, all packed with an amazing abundance of aquatic life.

The island is a haven for nature enthusiasts. It is easy to get around the eight-square-mile land area of St Eustatius, and many people take the opportunity to go hiking when here. The undisturbed interior offers excellent birding, and there are many well-marked that are lovingly maintained by the St Eustatius National Parks Foundation.

St Eustatius is, first and foremost, an excellent scuba diving destination. You can hire equipment from the *Golden Rock Dive Center*, which also provides full PADI instruction and certification. If you prefer, you can rent snorkeling equipment for an equally enjoyable, but vastly less expensive, underwater excursion. The company provides boat transportation to the best underwater sites.

St Eustatius is also a premier spot for hiking, due in part to the 2,000ft dormant volcano, known as the Quill. *Statia Holiday* offers guided tours through the mountainous rainforest and to the volcano summit. The firm provides transport to the Quill National Park from anywhere in the island, and lunch is provided. Visitors can also arrange daytrips to Boven National Park, a set of hills formed from ancient solidified lava. The park is also famed for its stunning views of nearby St Maarten Island, about 68 miles to the north.

The crater of the Quill provides excellent birding opportunities, with rare species such as the red necked pigeon and the purple throated

Carib regularly spotted. Visitors can contact *Stenapa* in Oranjestad to organize a ranger-led tour.

As St Eustatius is an island, there are plenty of opportunities to enjoy a day out on the Caribbean Sea. *Golden Rock* can arrange fishing excursions, or you can charter a boat for the day to experience the tranquil pleasures of independent seafaring. You can also book a ride on a power boat, departing from Oranjestad, with *Statia Holiday*. The company offers an around the island tour that allows guests to witness the island's splendor from the sparkling Caribbean Sea. The tour includes free drinks and snacks.

To experience all aspects of St Eustatius's natural splendor, take an island tour with *Statia Holiday*. The fully-guided excursion takes in the hills and remnants of the dormant Quill volcano in the north, the vast plains in the center of the island, and finishes with a trip to the south to see a more recently-formed volcano. Transport and lunch are provided.

Attractions

St Eustatius is a small and incredibly peaceful island, brimming with undisturbed natural beauty. The landscape in the south of the country is dominated by the Quill volcano, and climbing up to the crater is a popular visitor activity. On the walk there, visitors will encounter plenty of natural wonders, and many indigenous tropical plant specimens are preserved in the Miriam C Schmidt Botanic Gardens on the volcano's western slopes. St Eustatius also boasts a fascinating history; holidaymakers can learn more by joining one of the 600 archaeological digs each day, or by visiting the Historical Foundation Museum in Oranjestad.

The Quill
This dormant volcano was established as a national park in 1998, making it the first nationally protected ecological area in the Netherlands Antilles. Everything above 800ft is protected due to its unique biodiversity. Special vegetation, such as the Silk Cotton Tree and Trumpet Wood, flourishes at the crater of the volcano. At the highest point of the peak sits a rare elfin forest, and the crater is also home to a great deal of tropical birds. Unrivalled hiking and birding opportunities await on marked trails throughout the park. Address: The Quill National Park, southeastern St Eustatius Phone: n/a Website:http://www.statiapark.org/parks/quill/index.html

Miriam C Schmidt Botanical Gardens
The Miriam C Schmidt Botanical Gardens are the second National Park in St Eustatius, created in 1998. Many native flora species are prevalent here, and walking through the lush gardens makes for an

extremely pleasant pastime. There are also some sculptures by local artists on display here, and the park is famous for views of nearby St Kitts Island. The botanical gardens are committed to sustainability, and environmental education and conservation is a key focus. Address: Miriam C Schmidt Botanical Gardens, southeastern St Eustatius Phone:n/a Website: http://www.statiapark.org/parks/garden/index.html

Archaeological Sites

There are around 600 archaeological dig sites scattered around St Eustatius, all of which are protected by the St Eustatius Center for Archaeological Research (SECAR). The research is mainly focused on former slave life and culture, especially at locations such as the Lazaretto Leper Colony, Battery St Louis, the Godet Property, and the Godet Property. Everyone can contact SECAR and join the team at one of its excavations, for which they ask a small participation fee. Address: Archaeological sites, various. Website:http://www.secar.org

Oranjestad

Oranjestad is a historic harbor town, today home to 1,000 residents, which served as an important trade base with European nations during the 18th and 19th centuries. There are many beautifully restored historic buildings here, as well as atmospheric ruins set along the waterfront. The main historical site in town is Fort Oranje, a well maintained 17th century cliff-side fort complete with cannons pointing out to sea. There have also been modern developments in the town, however, and it is here where visitors will find the majority of the island's restaurants, retail stores, accommodations, and other services. Address: Oranjestad, southwestern St Eustatius

St Eustatius Historical Foundation Museum
St Eustatius is dubbed the 'historical gem' of the Caribbean, and this museum offers an insight into why this country has held such interest and significance in the region for so long. The museum, which is set in a preserved 18th century wealthy merchant's house, is open 9:00 a.m. to 5:00 p.m., Monday to Friday. Artifacts on display here range from pre-history to the colonial era. There is also a gallery, managed by the foundation and located nearby on Gallows Bay, showcasing historical artwork from the colonial period. The gallery is open between 9:00 a.m. and 12:00 p.m., Monday to Saturday. Address: St Eustatius Historical Foundation Museum, Oranjestad. Phone: +11-599-318-2288 Website: http://www.steustatiushistory.org/

Food and Restaurants

The island of St Eustatius does not really have its own specialized cuisine, but there are some tasty Creole (Caribbean of African descent) options for those looking for something a little exotic. The food here is mainly influenced by the Dutch, although visitors will find a whole host of international eateries, including European, American, and Asian. While on this stunning Caribbean island, visitors should take the opportunity to try some of the local seafood, such as pickled conch shell meat, grilled fish, and the ever-popular lobster. Most of the best restaurants are located in Oranjestad, the capital city, but meals vary wildly in price depending on location. However, no duty is imposed on imported foods, so most meals are fairly priced.

Bars and Pubbing in St Eustatius

Bars in St Eustatius boast a decidedly casual and laidback vibe, ensuring patrons never forget they're on a Caribbean island. Most of the bars are located in the capital city, Oranjestad, but elsewhere on the island alcohol can be purchased at restaurants or in local stores. There are no licensing laws on the island, although the reality is that most bars will close by midnight. If you are offered a greenie, don't be alarmed - this simply means a Heineken (Dutch beer).

Smoke Alley Bar & Grill (Gallows Bay, Lower Town) is an open-air beach bar, great for those looking to unwind and have a bite as the sun goes down. *Willy's Bar & Restaurant* (Helligerweg) is another vibrant nightspot, serving up both Spanish and local dishes. The *Original Fruit Tree* (Queen Beatrix Road) offers a different ambience and a slightly more upmarket atmosphere, as does *Cool Corner Bar & Restaurant*(Oranjestad). The latter is located in the heart of town and serves up great Chinese food. *Ocean View Terrace*(Oranjestad), situated on the edge of the bay, is a great place to unwind with a drink and admire the view.

Dining and Cuisine in St Eustatius

Chocolate Restaurant (Golden Rock, Oranjestad) is the place to go for traditional *Creole* dishes, while *Franky's Place* (Oranjestad Old Town) offers much of the same in a quiet location opposite the Methodist church. The *Golden Era Hotel* (Oranjestad Lower Town) also offers a Creole menu in a romantic setting overlooking the bay. The simply-named *Local Restaurant* (Paramiraweg) is another place you can sample some tasty Creole dishes, as well as freshly caught seafood. *Park View Restaurant* (Paramiraweg) also offers an extensive local menu and is known for its elegant use of goat meat, salt fish, and oxtail.

A nice option for breakfast is the *Old Gin House* (Oranjestad), set in a renovated 18th century cotton gin mill and only open in the mornings. *Sandbox Tree Bakery* (Oranjestad) is a good option for a light lunch with its vast selection of sandwiches and baked goods. *Sip & Zip Spanner Corner* (Helligerweg) also sells sandwiches and other snacks such as chicken wings and fried oxtail. *Opa's Snack* is another option for those looking to grab a quick bite.

There are also a few international options in Oranjestad. *Superburger* (Oranjestad), as the name suggests, offer burgers and other American-style food that can be washed down with hearty milkshakes. *Olde Towne Pizzeria* (Vantonningen) serves great Italian food, and is open from 6:00 p.m. until 10:00 p.m. every day but Friday. *Blue Bead Bar & Restaurant* (Gallows Bay) specializes in Italian and French cuisine, while *Sonny's Cantonese Restaurant* (Fort Oranjestad) serves up mouthwatering Chinese dishes, seven days a week.

Shopping and Leisure

St Eustatius is not known as a major shopping destination, as most products here are imported. However, no duty is charged on imports, so luxury items, such as perfume, jewelry, and alcohol, come much cheaper in St Eustatius than in neighboring Caribbean countries. Many restaurateurs travel over to the island from nearby St Kitts to grab a bargain, as even imported food is cheaper here. The capital of Oranjestad offers the best shopping, and is the major trading hub of the island. The usual shopping hours in St Eustatius are between 8:00 a.m. and 12:00 p.m., and then 2:00 p.m. until 6:00 p.m., but some stores close on Saturdays.

For souvenir shopping, head to Mazinga, which sells a range of products and books about St Eustatius from its location in Oranjestad Upper Town. The store is closed on weekends, but there is another branch (closed on Mondays and Tuesdays), set in a historic warehouse by the bay. Stenapa, located in Oranjestad Lower Town, is the main office of the National Parks Foundation of St Eustatius, and sells guidebooks, postcards, and souvenirs. For historical-related souvenirs, head for the St Eustatius Historical Foundation, which sells books, postcards, jewelry, artwork, and local vehicle number plates.

Lijfrock in Vannesweg is a wonderful jewelry store that stocks a mixture of imported goods and pieces made by local designers. Alois Boutique is a popular fashion store in Vantonningen, while surf wear and other apparel can be sourced from the Golden Rock Dive Center in Oranjestad Lower Town.

Paper Corner in Vantonnigen is a restored wooden rum shop, selling a selection of Caribbean rum and other liquor; however, shoppers should be aware that the rum is no longer made on St Eustatius itself. To purchase other food and drink items, go to one of the locally-owned supermarkets, such as Brown's Superette on Whitewall Road, or Duggind Supermarket and Department store in De Windtweg. For health food, look out for the Herb Center in Statia Mall.

Transportation

St Eustatius Taxis and Car Rental

Taxis are available on St Eustatius, based in the capital of Oranjestad. Taxis do not run on a meter but prices are fixed, set by the country's tourist office. You can pick up a copy of the price chart from the Statia Tourism Center in Oranjestad. The country is small, so it is possible to arrange a taxi to anywhere on the island, although some drivers have been known to refuse to drive on some of the poorly maintained roads in remote areas. Visitors can call *Ausvan Taxi* (+11-599-318-1300) or *Lijfrock* (+11-599-523-646) to arrange pickup.

Car rental is available via several locally-owned companies, such as *Brown's Car Rental* (+11-599-318-2266) and *Rainbow Car Rental* (+11-599-318-2811). Navigating St Eustatius is fairly easy since it is so small, but some of the roads are in need of repair. If you plan to go a remote area independently, it is worth renting an SUV.

St Eustatius Ferries

St Eustatius does not have domestic water taxis, but there is a scheduled ferry service to some of the two nearby islands in the Dutch Antilles group. The service, which only started in 2012, offers an alternative to making the trip by a 20-minute flight. The ferries run Monday to Friday and take around an hour and 30 minutes.

St Eustatius Trains and Buses

No rail network or public buses exist on St Eustatius. Sometimes private vehicles act as small buses for workers on fixed routes on the island, but the main way of getting around for visitors is by taxi or rental car. The island is just eight square miles across, meaning private transportation is fast and affordable. It only takes about an hour to travel the whole island by taxi or car, but you can also ask your hotel if they run minibus trips to other parts of the island, such as certain beaches or nature reserves.

Airports
Franklin D Roosevelt Airport
This airport is named after the 32nd President of the United States, whose ancestors lived on the island in the 18th century. St Eustatius was the first country to recognize the sovereignty of the newly independent USA in 1776. This amicable gesture was acknowledged by FDR during his visit to St Eustatius in 1939, and the country later they renamed the airport, originally called Black Rock, after the president.

The airport is small and does not currently accept scheduled international flights. The main way of reaching the island is by catching a connecting flight from the nearby island of St Maarten, which welcomes international flights from the US and Europe. The main destinations served by St Maarten Airport are Philadelphia, Charlotte, Paris, and Amsterdam.

The connecting flights from St Maarten are made by light, propeller powered aircraft, but the government is making plans to increase the runway by 1,000ft in order to allow for larger jets and an increase in destinations. The airport only has a small, single terminal building with very few services. It is located in Oranjestad, and is a short, 10-minute taxi ride from the downtown area.

Travel Tips

Language: Since St Eustatius was a former colony of, and today officially part of, the Netherlands, the official language is Dutch. However, most people on the island use English for everyday communication.

Currency
The local currency in St Eustatius is the Netherlands Antillean florin, also known as the Netherlands Antillean guilder. However, the US dollar is widely accepted, and it is worth bringing some with you to spend on holiday. There are very few ATMs on the island, so those wishing to withdraw money while away should ask for advance at a local bank. Banks are usually open between 8:00 a.m. and 4:00 p.m., Monday to Friday. Credit cards are widely accepted at hotels, shops,

and restaurants, but other smaller businesses may not have the facilities to accept credit cards.

Time: The time zone in St Eustatius is GMT -4:

Electricity
Electricity in St Eustatius runs at 110V/60Hz. You may need a transformer if your electrical appliances differ from this standard (most North American appliances run at 110-120 volts). They use two-pronged, flat North American-style plugs here, so you will need an adaptor for other types. Sockets will not accept a third 'grounding' pin, featured on UK plugs, so you will need an adaptor for these too.

Communications
The international calling code for St Eustatius +599. Cell phone reception is good in St Eustatius and, since the island is fairly small, you will get good coverage in most places. If your network does not offer international roaming, you can rent a cell phone from CelluarOne and connect to the local network. The island also has an excellent internet network, available in the majority of hotels and tourist spots.

Duty-free: If you are traveling to the US from St Eustatius, you are allowed to import one liter of alcohol and 200 cigarettes, 50 cigars, or 4lbs of tobacco. All these products are imported to St Eustatius and are available for the same price at any store on the island since no duty is levered on imports.

Tourist Office: St Eustatius Tourism Office: www.statiatourism.com

Consulates in St Eustatius: There is no diplomatic representation on the island of St Eustatius. The closest consulates in nearby countries are:

American Consulate, Curacao: +11-599-9461-3066

Canadian Consulate, St Maarten: +11-599-543-6261

British Consulate, Curacao: +11-599-9747-3322

Emergency: Police: 911 Medical: 912 Fire: 913

Visas and Vaccinations

St Eustatius is a special municipality of the Netherlands, so the same rules apply as if visiting the mainland in Europe. American, Canadian, Australian, and New Zealand citizens do not need a visa and will be automatically granted 90-day tourist access on arrival. Visitors from Britain and other EU states also do not need a visa. In order to enter St Eustatius, you are required to have six months validity on your passport and a return ticket.

Health and Safety

St Eustatius has an excellent public health record, and visitors have a low-level risk of contracting most diseases. However, it is recommended you seek the following routine vaccinations before you travel: hepatitis A and B, MMR, and typhoid. If your vaccines are not up to date, you should renew six to eight weeks before your intended travel date. You may wish to also get a rabies vaccination if you intend to be in close proximity of bats. There is no malaria on the island and no reports of Dengue fever; both which are spread by mosquitoes. In any case, it is recommended that visitors use mosquito repellent to defend against bites.

St Eustatius is an extremely safe country, with a small and friendly population. However, usual precautions should be taken to defend against crime. Bag snatching can has been known in the country, and it is best to not carry large amounts of cash, jewelry, and your passport. You should leave all valuables in the safe in your hotel.

Being a tropical country, St Eustatius is at risk of violent storms, especially during the hurricane season that lasts from June to November each year. St Eustatius has experienced some severe hurricanes over the last decade, so if you are travelling somewhere remote during the hurricane season, it is best to check weather reports or visit the US National Hurricane Center website: http://www.nhc.noaa.gov/

Weather

St Eustatius is a humid tropical island, with temperatures averaging 80°F throughout the year. There is little variation in the seasons, but temperatures never exceed 85°F. Temperatures drop by about 10°F during the nights, which can feel chilly after a day in the sun. The climate is moderated by cool trade winds coming from the northeast. The coldest temperatures on the island can be experienced on St Eustatius's highest peak, which reaches 1,950ft.

The rainy season in Martinique runs between August and December, seeing up to 6.5 inches of rain in the wettest month of September compared with only 2.5 inches in March during the dry season. April and June also experience heavy showers, but these are generally short-lived. Throughout the year you can expect at least eight hours of sunshine every day, although there is still around of thirteen days of rain showers, even in the driest months. If travelling to exposed areas, light wet weather gear is recommended.

The hurricane season on St Eustatius usually runs from June to October. The island has suffered a few direct hits from tropical cyclones over the last 10 years. Advanced storm warning systems are used on the island, however, to keep residents and visitors informed and safe.

Best Time to Visit St Eustatius

As, temperatures remain constant throughout the year in St Eustatius, the best time to holiday here is determined by humidity and rain. Most visitors to St Eustatius chose to go during the dry season, with the best months being December through to April. After this time, the air becomes humid and sticky before the rains begin to break in August.

Hotel prices do not vary through the year, so those seeking a vacation during the high season, between December and April, will find St Eustatius offers good value for money when other islands in the region tend to double their rates.

Accommodations can get booked up towards the end of July when people flock to the island to celebrate the annual carnival; booking a hotel well in advance is recommended during this time. According to historic weather patterns, the most likely week for a hurricane to hit St Eustatius is in the middle of September, so you may wish to avoid planning a visit at this time if that's a concern.

Holidays and Festivals

St Eustatius is a country with both a proud Caribbean heritage and strong links to its motherland of the Netherlands. For example, one of the biggest St Eustatius holidays is Emancipation Day, which celebrates the end of slavery in the Caribbean, while another big day is Queen's Day, which celebrates the figureheads of the Dutch monarchy. The dominant religion is Catholicism, so Christian holidays such as Easter and Christmas are also important.

Easter Monday
Usually held in April, but flexible according to the Christian calendar, this event sees island-wide beach picnics with delicious food and drink, accompanied by typical 'Statia' music.

Queen's Day
Held annually on April 30 to commemorate the former Dutch Queen Juliana, this celebration involves cross island cultural events, beach picnics, and music. Islanders wear something bright orange to mark their allegiance to the Dutch nation.

Emancipation Day
This festival marks the abolition of slavery, an important milestone for Caribbean countries. Locals celebrate the event by wearing traditional costume and dancing traditional steps. Music starts at 6:00 a.m. on July 1 and lasts all day.

Carnival
Running since 1964, this annual festival is held in the last week of July. It takes a similar form to other Caribbean carnivals, with people dressing up in colorful costumes for parades and pageants in the streets. The festival continues into the night, and the air is filled with the sound of Calypso music.

Golden Rock Regatta
This week-long sailing event is held annually on the second week of November. It attracts sailors from around the world who come to race yachts in the Caribbean. The competitions sail around St Eustatius and to other nearby islands.

Statia Day
This national holiday commemorates the fact that St Eustatius was the first in the world to recognize the independence of USA. Today, residents use the event to celebrate the history and culture of St Eustatius in general. Throughout the week leading up to the day, uniformed groups parade through the streets bearing the flag of St Eustatius. Nightly performances, demonstrating modern Eustatiun principals, are also enjoyed in public areas

Sint Maarten

About St Maarten

Sun-lovers, water babies, sailors and divers alike will find St Maarten an alluring Caribbean getaway. This popular destination in the former Netherlands Antilles is lined with delicious coastline, on which to frolic, bake, or get active.

The most prominent physical feature in St Maarten is Mount Flagstaff, an extinct volcano, but the most important for visitors is the excellent beach that follows the south and west coasts; beach activities and shopping at duty-free centres firmly satisfy most tourists.

St Maarten is also popular with sailing enthusiasts and divers. The excellent diving conditions feature striking coral reefs located close to the shore. One of the most popular dive sites is the wreck of HMS Proselyte, a British man-of-war which sank in 1801. Body boarding is increasingly popular way of enjoying the gleaming waters and getting refreshed in the pouring sunshine

History and Culture

St Martin was squabbled over by colonial powers for decades before being peacefully divided between the French and Dutch, resulting in the unique border relationship these two nations maintain to the present day. Visitors will see many cultural influences on both sides of the island, with everything from French haute cuisine to the Dutch language on show in this unique Caribbean nation.

History

The first European to sight St Maarten was Christopher Columbus on his expedition of 1493. He named it St Martin, after St Martin of Tours, since the day he first saw the island was November 11, which is a celebration of the saint. Columbus immediately claimed the island for the Spanish, although he never landed.

Once St Maarten had been mapped, the Dutch and French took great interest in it. The Dutch saw it as a good point along the way to link their colonies in America, known then as New Amsterdam (which is modern day New York), and their settlements in Brazil at the time. The French had colonies in Trinidad and Bermuda, and wanted to colonize the islands in between.

St Maarten remained largely uninhabited until the Dutch formally founded a settlement in 1631, erecting Fort Amsterdam on the headland between Little and Great Bay in the south of the island, near modern day Philipsburg. The Dutch East India Company then began salt mining operations on the island, and as a result of British and then further French interest, the Spanish took heed and decided to exert authority over their claim from 1493.

Spain and the Netherlands were enemies at the time, and fought battles over a long period called the "Eighty Years" War' between 1568 and 1648. Spanish forces attacked and captured the island of St Martin in 1633, but after defending it against the Dutch forces who wished to reclaim it, they eventually deserted the island after 15 years in 1648.

With St Maarten up for the taking, both the Dutch and French swept in to make claims. There was initial conflict, but then preferring a peaceful negotiation both sides, the two nations signed the Treaty of Concordia in 1648, officially dividing the island in two. For the next 170 years, small conflicts changed the border 16 times, until the present day boundary was established.

However, the border has never really been enforced, and islanders have always been free to roam both sides, a benefit also available to tourists today. By the middle of the 20th century, the government of St Maarten decided to shift its main economic focus toward tourism, an aspect which has grown and is now making the country a major tourist destination. This has had a huge impact on the demographics and cultural make up of the country since the population rose from 5,000 people up to 80,000 people by the mid-1990s, with most of the immigrants coming from the nearby Caribbean countries of Curacao, Haiti, and the Dominican Republic, as well as people from USA, Europe, and Asia.

Culture

The culture of St Maarten is a mixture of Dutch, French, British, and African heritage. Even though St Maarten and French St Martin are different countries, they share a similar history and heritage. Today, all school children on both sides are taught to be tri-lingual in Dutch, English, and French. The native 'Creole' population can trace their roots to Africa since their ancestors were brought here as slaves to work on the plantations.

You can gain a better insight into the intriguing cultural mix on this tiny island by visiting the St Maarten Museum in Philipsburg. It has exhibits covering the rich heritage of St Maarten and the island of St Martin as a whole.

Travel and Tourism

Travel Guide

St Maarten constitutes the southern half of the island of St Martin, in the eastern Caribbean. Officially, the island is the smallest in the world ever to have been divided between two different nations. St Maarten is the Dutch side, and the northern side is French. The two nations have managed to share their border in the spirit of cooperation and mutual friendship for around 350 years. The entire island is only 37 square miles in total area, and with a visit here you will be able to see for yourself just what makes it so special that two competing nations staked a claim for this gem in the Caribbean Sea.

Beach tourism is undoubtedly the main draw of the island, and with so many picture-perfect white sandy beaches lapped with crystal clear warm waters, there is a good reason why. There are many water sports on offer here, such as scuba diving, waterskiing, and surfing. Also, boating activities provide a great way to experience the Caribbean, with many people choosing to charter a yacht or go on a boat tour or fishing excursion.

There are several places to stay on the island, built to western standards. Tourism has been developed in St Maarten since the middle of last century, and today there are many resort-style accommodations to choose from at marvelous locations overlooking the beach. St Maarten is also home to many purpose-built spas, some of which are part of top class hotel resorts providing a complete package. Dining options are varied and equally well catered for, with many high quality restaurants established here.

Beaches around St Maarten are well known to be some of the best in the world; you could easily spend a day at each one during a visit here. It is easy to see what life is like on the other side in French St Martin since there is no border control and you can drive between the two major cities in about 30 minutes. Here, you can witness a slightly more Gallic way of life, as opposed to the Dutch influences, although the entire island is unified in that English is the main language.

St Maarten is a tropical country on an island in the Caribbean Sea with very constant. In the coldest month of February, you can expect temperatures between 72-82°F. The warmest month is August, when you can expect temperatures between 78-87°F. Precipitation is fairly regular in St Maarten, and the country does not really experience a rainy season. Between mid-November and mid-April, St Maarten experiences regular trade winds blowing from the northeast, which has a pleasant cooling effect. During the summer months, the wind can be more forceful, bringing in heavy rain showers, although these showers do not last for long.

The international airport serving both sides is located in St Maarten, about 20 minutes' drive west of the capital city, Philipsburg. Taxis are plentiful and willing to take you anywhere on both sides of the island, while car rental is an option. The island is small, so to circumnavigate your way round will only take about an hour, although there are many amazing beaches along the way that will catch your eye.

Things to Do

It is not surprising that St Maarten makes the most of its wonderful location on an island in the Caribbean Sea, and with year-round water temperatures averaging 80°F, it makes a great diving and snorkeling destination. There are plenty of other water sports on offer, such as windsurfing and waterskiing, and many people like to experience the Caribbean by boat, either a by chartering a yacht or letting someone else be skipper on a boat cruise. If you prefer dry land and love nature then you will enjoy a birding tour to try and spot one of the 150 species that call St Maarten their home.

With the amazing clear blues seas of the Caribbean and plenty of sunlight filtering through to explore the underwater world, St Maarten is an excellent scuba diving destination. *Octopus Diving* offers equipment rental and dive excursions to 30 sites around the island. It also offers full PADI certification courses. If full scuba diving is not for you, then you can join a snorkeling excursion.

Quite possibly there is nothing better to do when in St Maarten than to set sail on the Caribbean Sea, and you can charter a yacht from *Sunsail*. You will need to head over to Oyster Pond on the French side in order to collect the boat.

A great way of experiencing the Caribbean Sea is to take a boat cruise around the island, and you can go with *Aqua Mania Adventures*, which provides complete day packages, including lunch.

There are several other water sports options on St Maarten, such as waterskiing, windsurfing, and wave running. *Simpson Bay Resort* has the largest water sports center and equipment rental choice in St Maarten, including the rental of ocean kayaks.

The Caribbean waters around St Maarten are bountiful for game fishing, with marlin, dorado, sailfish, and tuna swimming in the sea. *Rudy's Deep Sea Fishing* offers several fishing excursions, from those suited to novice to expert fishers.

Nature lovers will be satisfied with the ample birding available on St Maarten since it is home to around 150 species. *St Maarten Bird Foundation* provides group educational tours, taking you to the best spots on the island, as well as tailor-made packages to suit your needs.

A thrilling way to experience the island is to rent a motorbike or a quad bike. *Harley Davidson Rental and Tour* offers rental of the touring bikes for the day, and *Solid ATV* offers rental of quad-bikes for you to explore the rugged areas of the island.

Offering an exotic and unforgettable experience for you and your guests, getting married on St Maarten is popular. *St Maarten Marry-Me* provides complete wedding packages and can help assist with all arrangements to make it a truly special day to be remembered.

Attractions

Occupying the lower half of the Caribbean island of St Martin, St Maarten offers beautiful sandy beaches that feature highly as places to go in the country. Some are located on the eastern side, and with the next continental landmass being Africa, heading here at the start of the day to watch the sunrise over the ocean is an awe-inspiring experience. South-facing beaches provide great surf. Inland, there are a few attractions, including a tropical zoo, and there is a historical border monument to discover.

Cupecoy Beach: Imagine a picture-postcard ideal of a white sand beach awash with turquoise sea and you have arrived at Cupecoy. Dominated by white cliffs that tower over it, the beach at Cupecoy is simply stunning and a great place to relax for the day, with sunbathing interspersed with dips into the sea. There are also caves you can explore when the tide is out. Address: Cupecoy Beach, Western St Maarten

Guana Bay Beach: Located very close to the capital at Philipsburg, this wide and shallow bay is a great spot for body boarding and surfing. It is a quiet and relaxing beach, away from the big resorts that dominate other coastal areas of St Maarten Address: Guana Bay Beach, Eastern St Maarten.

Dawn Beach: As its name may suggest, this is an excellent spot to watch the sunrise as its shore faces the east. It is also a popular snorkeling spot since there is a wonderful coral reef to be admired off the shore. Address: Dawn Beach, Oyster Pond, Eastern St Maarten

St Maarten Zoo: A visit to this zoo, which houses over 60 species of animals, is a great day out. It features many tropical birds, mammals, and reptiles; many of which are rare and endangered. There is also a dedicated bird walk through the aviaries. Address: St Maarten Zoo, Great Salt Pond, central St Maarten Phone: +11-721-543-2030 Website: http://www.stmaartenzoo.com:

Mullet Bay Beach: This beach has the best waves, making it a popular destination for surfers. There are a few places to eat and drink nearby, while the moon-shaped bay is also close to the island's only golf course. Address: Mullet Bay Beach, Western St Maarten Mayreau.

St Maarten Museum: This museum is managed by the St Maarten National Heritage Foundation and provides information on many aspects of the island's natural and cultural history. It includes the history of the island's geological formation, details on the original Arawak inhabitants, and colonial history, including slavery. Address: St Maarten Museum, Front Street, Philipsburg Phone: +11-721-542-4917 Website:http://www.museumsintmaarten.org/

Border Monument: This monument was erected in 1948 to commemorate 300 years of coexistence between French St Martin and Dutch St Maarten, which share the island. It is located at the border, where even though a partition treaty was signed in 1648, there was no clear delineation until 1772. You will pass this monument if you take the road from Cole Bay to Marigot. Address: Union Road, central St Maartenl

Holidays and Festivals

St Maarten is part of an island in the Caribbean Sea and the inhabitants are proud of their nation's location. Annual boating events, such as the Regatta held in March and the Alliance Race held in November, are popular events that attract many international visitors. The spring Carnival is a big St Maarten holiday, and is celebrated simultaneously on both sides of the island. It is worth stepping over to the French side at this time to take a look at the differences in celebration, albeit both sides party in true Caribbean style.

Regatta
This is a three-day boat race held in March every year. The first day sees a race around the island, and then there are special courses designed on the second and third days. At the end of each racing event, the day is closed with a celebration party. The event attracts sailors from around the globe to compete.

Carnival
This festival goes on for three weeks, commencing in the middle of April and finishing at the first weekend of May. It is celebrated on both sides of St Maarten, although on the Dutch side the grand parade happens in the capital city, where people dressed in flamboyant

Caribbean costumes dance through the streets to the sounds of soca and calypso music.

Grand Case Festival
This festival takes place on July 21 every year and sees families come together to commemorate the abolition of slavery. Slavery was officially abolished in 1833, and events prior to and since have had a huge effect on the history and cultural make-up of this Caribbean society.

St Maarten Day
Also known as Martinmas, this festival celebrates St Martin of Tours and is a traditional time for feasting celebrations. St Martin Island, which St Maarten is a part of, was named so by Christopher Columbus because he spotted the country on this saint's feast day in 1493. The festival is celebrated on November 11 and is a public holiday so most stores close.

Flavors of St Maarten Food & Wine Festival
Held in November and celebrated with growing popularity is this showcase of the island's top chefs and their signature dishes. The festival's locations vary, although the boardwalk in Philipsburg hosts a large array of events.

Alliance Race

This is another major racing event on St Maarten's sailing calendar. The boats commence the race from Simpson Bay in St Maarten, setting sail for St Barts and then on to Anguilla before returning to Margot Bay in French St Martin to cross the finish line.

Food and Restaurants

Even though St Maarten is a very small country, perhaps the most interesting thing about the food here is that you can sample some the world's best cuisine, from France, the Netherlands, Italy, India, Japan, Thailand, and Vietnam. Of course, it would be impossible for the restaurants to not offer typical Caribbean food, and since St Maarten is a country on an island, fresh fish and seafood are always on the menu. There are many options to suit all budgets, and restaurants in St Maarten always leave diners satisfied with the quality of food served. Away from the formal restaurants, you could try grabbing a meal at one of the *lolos*. These venues are local food stalls at roadsides selling delicious barbecued meats and fish, which are served with spicy Caribbean sauces.

Bars and Pubbing in St Maarten

St Maarten has a great atmosphere, but limited nightlife. For better options, you may want to head over to *Grand Case* on the French side of the island. But in St Maarten you can try *Tantra Nightclub & Sanctuary* (1 Rhine Road, Maho Bay), located at the Sonesta Resort & Casino. This is a true nightclub in that sense that things do not really get going until about 1:00 a.m., although the action continues until at least 6:00 a.m. If you go to French St Martin, you can try *Boo Boo Jam* (Baie Orientale, St Martin) or *La Noche* (Grand Case, St Martin), which both play modern electronic music.

Simpson Bay has a cluster of bars, such as *Bliss* (Caravansernal Resort, Simpson Bay), which has a roof-top lounge to enjoy a drink until late into the night. Behind Atrium Beach resort you will find *Bucaneer Bar* (10 Billy Folly Road, Simpson Bay), a friendly place where you can relax over a 'BBC' cocktail (Bailey's banana colada).

St Maarten also has several casinos for anyone feeling lucky. Philipsburg has the most, for example *Diamond Casino* (1 Front Street, Philipsburg), which has 250 slot machines, roulette, and card tables. *Coliseum* and *Beach Plaza Casino* offer similar experiences; both are located at Front Street in Philipsburg. If in Maho Bay, you can try *Casino Royale* (1 Rhine Road, Maho).

Dining and Cuisine in St Maarten

For the biggest choice of restaurants in St Maarten, you should head to Philipsburg. A popular restaurant here serving typical Caribbean food is *Chesterfield's* (Great Bay Marina, Philipsburg), which specializes in seafood dishes. *Ocean Lounge* (43 Front Street, Philipsburg) offers fresh fish and seafood dishes, matched by a great view over the marina.

For French cuisine, the best in town is usually considered to be *Antoine* (119 Front Street, Philipsburg), which is famous for dishes such as *lobster thermidor* (lobster cooked with cream and Swiss cheese), or you could try *L'Escargot* (96 Front Street, Philipsburg), which provides entertainment by way of a cabaret show on Friday nights.

Maho Beach and Simpson Bay also provide a cluster of restaurants. *Big Fish* (14 Emerald Merrit Road, Maho Beach) provides fresh seafood dishes cooked with Caribbean flavorings, such as coconut milk and local spices. *The Boathouse* (74 Airport Road, Simpson Bay) and *Pineapple Pete* (56 Welfare Rd., Simpson Bay) are seafood restaurants in the Simpson Bay area. Around both Maho and Simpson Bay you will also find Italian, French, and Asian dining options.

Shopping and Leisure

St Maarten is heralded as being a shopper's delight in the Caribbean, with lower prices than any other country in the Caribbean. Both the

Dutch and French sides of the island have duty-free prices, so there is no sales tax paid by buyers. This provides an extremely competitive shopping environment for luxury goods, such as jewelry, cosmetics, electronics, alcohol, and tobacco. Prices are around 15-30 percent cheaper than in the US for these products.

The main shopping area in St Maarten is Front Street in Philipsburg. Here, you will find a mile-long strip of stores selling luxury products at competitive, duty-free prices. For clothing and general souvenirs, a good place to head is Back Street, which sells beachwear and island memorabilia.

All around this area of Philipsburg you will find food and snacks to buy, including at the open-air bazaar located behind the courthouse, which is nestled in between Front and Back streets. Stores are normally open seven days per week, from 9:00 a.m. until 6:00 p.m., with a two-hour closing for lunch between 12:00 p.m. and 2:00 p.m.

There is a branch of Cartier located at 35 Front Street, or for luxury watches and jewelry from Bell & Ross, and Pomellato, you can go to Carat at 73 Front Street. There is also a branch of Tommy Hilfiger and Ralph Lauren clothing stores on Front Street at numbers 28 and 31 respectively. There is an endearing souvenir shop at 8 Front Street called Guavaberry Emporium which sells items such as hand-painted bottles and liquor.

Spas and Wellness

With an amazing location and a tranquil setting, St Maarten is an extremely popular spa retreat for visitors. There are several spas located in the country, usually near the south-facing beaches. Some of the most popular include the Dawn Beach Resort & Spa near the airport, the Christian Dior Spa at the Cliff Hotel, and Serenity Spa at Maho Beach Resort. There are plenty of other options, including the Good Life Spa and Spa St Maarten at Little Bay Beach Resort and Oyster Bay Beach Resort. It may also be worth heading over to the French side of St Martin where more options are available, such as La Samanna and Radisson Blu Resort & Spa.

Transportation

St Maarten Taxis and Car Rental

There are plenty of taxis in St Maarten, which are usually vans which can carry up to 10 people. It is possible to use taxis to access both the Dutch and French sides as there is no need to go through any border controls. Circumnavigating the entire island takes about an hour, and many taxis are willing to be rented for the entire day to take you on a tour of the island. You can call the *Dutch St Maarten Taxi Association* (+11-721-543-7815) to book.

There are several car rental companies located at the airport in St Maarten, and self-driving is popular here. Many of the roads are narrow and some are in bad condition so extra care should be taken when driving here. You can call *Avis* (+11-721-552-2847), *Budget* (+11-721-545-4030), or *Hertz* (+11-721-554-314), which have a range of vehicles on offer.

St Maarten Water Taxis

There are water taxis available to shuttle passengers between Philipsburg to the cruise ship docking area. Both single trip tickets and wrist bands which will cover multiple trips in a single day are available.

St Maarten Trains and Buses

There are no trains in St Maarten. The only form of public transportation is privately owned vans, regulated by the government, which operate as buses. You will be able to recognize these vehicles because their license plates read the word 'BUS'. There are frequent routes between Philipsburg and Marigot (on the French side), as well as other places.

Airports

Princess Juliana International Airport

The only international airport serving the island of St Martin is Princess Juliana, in St Maarten, so it is shared by visitors to both sides of the island. There is joint border control and customs with the Dutch and French authorities. The airport sees over 1.6 million passengers every year, with direct flights to the US destinations of Atlanta, Chicago, Miami, New York-JFK, Newark, and Washington Dulles with American Airlines, Delta, and United Airlines. There are also currently several budget airlines operating between the US and St Maarten. For Canadian destinations, Air Canada and CanJet provide services from Montreal and Toronto, although some flights are only operational in the high season. To come from Europe, the only airline operating a direct flight is KLM from Amsterdam.

The airport is modern since it has been recently upgraded. There are many passenger services in the terminal building, such as over 40 retail stores and restaurants, including duty-free stores. The airport is located on a thin strip of land between Simpson Bay and Simpson Lagoon. Because of this location, it is particularly popular with aviation enthusiasts as planes fly right over Maho Beach, providing an extremely close encounter from below. However, plane-spotting here is not for the faint hearted as the rumbling bellows of the jet engines may knock you off balance and temporarily deafen you. The airport is located about six miles west of Philipsburg, a maximum 20 minute journey away. Taxis are readily available at the airport to take you anywhere on the island or there are several car rental agencies.

Travel Tips

Language: The official languages of St Maarten are Dutch and English. On the French side of St Martin, French is the official language, but English is widely spoken. School children on both sides of the island are now educated in Dutch, English, French, and Spanish, so the island is multilingual.

Currency: The official currency of St Maarten is the Netherlands Antilles guilder, also known as the florin, although in effect most businesses gladly accept US dollars and euro so there is no need to exchange these currencies for use in the country. The Netherlands Antilles guilder is due to be replaced by the Caribbean guilder in 2013, although it is expected that the practice of accepting US dollars and euro from tourists will continue.

Time: The time zone in St Maarten is GMT -4.

Electricity: Electricity in St Maarten runs at 110-120V/60Hz. You may need a transformer if your electrical appliance differs from this standard (most North American appliances run at 110-120V). European style, rounded two-pin electrical socket are in use here. You will need an adaptor if your plug does not meet these standards. In addition, if visiting the French side, take note that electricity runs at 250V/50Hz, so you will need a currency transformer to use items that are designed to be used on the Dutch side (or you may be able to borrow one from your hotel).

Communications: The international calling code for St Maarten is +721. You may see this code on old advertisements and notices displayed as +599, with the former code having expired in 2012. Cell phone communication is excellent in St Maarten and is available in most places across both sides of the island. If you have international roaming on your phone, you can connect to the local network, or you can enquire about renting a phone at the airport or your hotel. St Maarten also has good high-speed internet available in the majority of hotels and tourist spots.

Duty-free: Duty-free goods can be purchased at St Maarten. If you are traveling to the US, you are allowed to import one liter of alcohol and 200 cigarettes, 50 cigars, or four pounds of tobacco. There is a mile-long duty-free shopping street in the capital, Philipsburg, with a good range of jewelry and perfumery.

Tourist Office: St Maarten Tourism Bureau: www.en.vacationstmaarten.com/

Consulates in St Maarten: There is no diplomatic representation of the US in St Maarten. The closest consular section is in the nearby country of Curacao. The same applies for Britain, although Canada has its nearest consulate in Trinidad and Tobago:

US Embassy, Curacao: +11-599-9461-3066 British Consulate, Curacao: +11-599-9461-3900 Canadian Consulate, Trinidad and Tobago: +11-868-622-6232 British Honorary Consul, St Vincent and the Grenadines: +11-784-457-6860

Emergency: Emergency services: 911

Visas and Vaccinations

US citizens do not need a visa for a stay of up to 90 days. Visitors from EU countries, Australia, and New Zealand are also visa exempt. Visitors from these countries will be granted a 90-day stay for tourist purposes on arrival, although they are required to have at least six months' validity on their passport and possess a return ticket.

Health and Safety

There is no risk of yellow fever in St Maarten; however, a certificate is required to enter the country if you have visited an at-risk area within the previous week. If you have visited an infected area and do not possess a valid yellow fever certificate, you should seek a vaccine eight weeks before you travel. It is recommended that you also seek the following routine vaccinations before you travel: hepatitis A, diphtheria, MMR, and tetanus. If your vaccines are not up to date, you should renew six to eight weeks before your intended travel date. There is no risk of malaria on St Martin Island, although it is recommended to use mosquito repellent and to cover up exposed skin at night in order to defend against insect bites.

St Maarten is an extremely safe country, and incidences of crime against tourists are rare, although they are reported on occasion. Most common are muggings and thefts from hotels and yachts, occasionally accompanied by violence if met with resistance. It is best not to resist any muggings, and you should avoid walking alone in isolated areas at night, including beaches.

Being in the tropics, St Maarten is at risk of violent storms, and hurricane season lasts from June to November each year. If traveling somewhere remote in St Maarten during this season, it is best to check weather reports or visit the US National Hurricane Center website.

Weather

St Maarten is a tropical country on an island in the Caribbean Sea. Temperatures do not fluctuate much here. In the coldest month of February, you can expect temperatures of between 72-82°F, and in the warmest month of August, you can expect temperatures between 78-87°F. Precipitation is fairly regular in St Maarten, and the country does not really experience a rainy season. The driest month is March, which sees about 1.5 inches of rainfall, and the wettest month is October, which see about 4.5 inches of rain.

Between mid-November and mid-April, St Maarten experiences regular trade winds blowing from the northeast, which has a pleasant cooling effect. During the summer months, the wind can be more forceful, bringing in heavy rain showers, although these showers do not last for long. Temperatures of the surrounding Caribbean waters range from 78-80°F in the winter to 82-84°F in the summer.

St Maarten is located within the Atlantic hurricane belt. The last major cyclone hit in 1995. Advanced warning systems are in place for people's safety, although visitors should expect storms during the hurricane season. The official hurricane season is between June and November, which coincides with the wet season. However, St Maarten has only experienced two major hurricanes in over 50 years.

Best Time to Visit St Maarten

Mid-December to May is the typical high season in St Maarten. Hotels lower their rates by around 50 percent in May and June and November to December, so these periods may be good times to visit, while the weather is still pleasant and not affected by the hurricane season. Many hotels actually close during the hurricane season, from June/July until late October.

The weather is best between December and May, although accommodation needs to be booked at least two months in advance during this period. Christmas, Martin Luther King, and President's Day long weekends are the busiest times for St Maarten. Visiting between November and mid-December means visitors will experience the same weather as peak period but at reduced prices.

www.ingramcontent.com/pod-product-compliance
Lightning Source LLC
Chambersburg PA
CBHW021101080526
44587CB00010B/334